A STRAIGHTFORWARD GUIDE TO THE RIGHTS OF THE PRIVATE TENANT

ROGER SPROSTON BA MSc

Straightforward Publishing
www.straightforwardbooks.co.uk

Straightforward Guides

ISBN

978-1-80236-425-5

Printed by 4edge www.4edge.co.uk

Cover design by BW Studio Derby

Publisher: Straightforward Publishing, Derby, United Kingdon
EU Authorised Representative: Easy Access System Europe-Mustamae tee 50 10621 Tallin, Estonia,
gpsr.requests@easproject.com

CONTENTS

Introduction

The Renters Rights Bill 2024

Ch. 1- Tenants-Looking for Property-Using Letting Agents 33

Letting Agents 33

Online lettings agents 34

Responsibilities of lettings agents 34

Immigration Act 2014 and checking eligibility to rent 35

Discrimination against tenants on housing benefits 36

The lettings process -Pre-tenancy checks 36

Payments at the start of the tenancy 37

How to rent guide 38

Deposits-Tenancy Deposit Protection Scheme 38

Moving into a property 38

The Deregulation Act 2015 41

Rental guarantees 41

Chapter 2-General Information about Types of Lettings 43

Company lets 43

Short lets 43

Student lets 44

Holiday lets 45

Bedsits 45

Landlords taking in a lodger 46

Letting through Airbnb 47
Kindroom 48

Ch. 3-Private Housing Issues for the Disabled 50
Generally 50
Making adaptations to a property 51
Minor adaptations 53
Major adaptations 53
Funding and access 54

Ch. 4-Basic Elements of the Law in a Nutshell 55
Explaining the law 55
The freehold and the lease 56
Freehold 56
Leasehold 56
The position of the tenant 57
The tenancy agreement 57
The contract 58
Date of commencement of tenancy and rent payable 58
Services provided under the tenancy and service of notice 59
Tenants' obligations 59
Landlords' obligations 59
Ending a tenancy 59
Key features of the Renters Rights Bill 2024 61
The responsibility of the landlord to provide a rent book 63
Overcrowding 63
Different types of tenancy agreement 63

The protected tenancy - the meaning of the term 64
The assured shorthold tenancy - what it means 64

Ch. 5-Joint Tenancies 69
Joint tenancies 69
Tenancy agreements 69
Right to rent 69
Paying the rent when you're a joint tenant 69
Tenancy deposits 70
Tenancy deposits when a joint tenant moves out 70
How you can end a fixed-term joint tenancy 70
How to end a joint tenancy that isn't a fixed-term 71
Leaving a joint tenancy 71
Eviction of joint tenants 72
Relationship breakdown 72
Problems with other joint tenants 72

Ch. 6-The Payment of Rent and Other Charges 73
The payment of rent and other financial matters 73
The assured tenant 73
Local housing allowance (LHA) (housing benefit) for people who rent a home from a private landlord. 74
Claiming LHA 74
How LHA is calculated 75
Maximum LHA amounts 75
Rooms allowed when calculating LHA 75
If you're aged under 35 76

How often is housing benefit paid? 76
When LHA can be paid direct to landlords 77
Council Tax Support 77

Ch. 7-The Right to Quiet Enjoyment of a Home 79
Eviction: what can be done against unlawful eviction 79
Remedies for unlawful eviction 81
The injunction 81
Damages 82

Ch.8 Repairs-Landlords and Tenants Obligations 83
Repairs and improvements generally: The landlord and tenants' obligations 83
Implied standards of fitness for human habitation 84
AWAABS Law 84
The Housing Health and Safety rating System (HHSRS) 85
What is a hazard? 85
What happens when a hazard is discovered? 86
Example of general repairs a landlord is responsible for 87
Reporting repairs to landlords 88
The tenants' rights whilst repairs are being carried out 88
Can the landlord put the rent up after doing repairs? 89
Tenants' rights to make improvements to a property 89
Disabled tenants 89
Houses in multiple occupation (HMO) 90
Extra responsibilities of HMO landlords 91
Responsibility for repairs in HMOs 91

Landlord penalties for not having an HMO licence 93
Safety generally for all landlords 93
Minimising risks in a rental property 94
Items supplied in rental property 95
Fire Safety Regulations in Rental Property 95
Do landlords need to fit a smoke alarm in rental property 96
Smoke and carbon monxide alarm requirements 96
What happens if Landlords don't comply? 96
What type of smoke alarm should I install? 96
Responsibility for testing and maintaining the fire alarms 97
Fire Extinguishers in a Rental Property 97
Gas safety 98
Furniture Safety 98
Regulations -Furniture and Furnishings in Rental Property 98
Compliance with the regulations on furniture 99
Electrical Safety 100
Obligations-Landlords to upgrade and maintain insulation 102
The availability of grants 103
Legionnaire's disease 103
Sanitation health and hygiene generally 105

Ch. 9-What Should Be Provided Under a Tenancy 107
Furniture 107
Insurance 108
At the end of the tenancy 108
A word on inventories 109

Ch. 10-Landlord Taking Possession of a Property **111**
Accelerated (Fast-track) possession 112
Rules for Section 21 notices 112
Section 21 (Form 6A) pre-requisites 112
Going to court to end the tenancy 115
Ending your tenancy legally 117
Giving notice to your landlord 118
Agreeing to end the tenancy 118

Ch. 11-Private Tenancies in Scotland **119**
The Housing Bill (Scotland) 2024 119
The law generally in Scotland 122
The Private Residential Tenancy-Scotland 122
Person already an assured/short assured tenant 124
What is a private residential tenancy? 124
Tenancy agreements 124
Bringing a tenancy to an end 125
Ending a tenancy 123
Landlord access 126
Getting repairs carried out 126
Passing tenancy on to someone else 126
Tenancies that cannot be a private residential tenancy 127
Short assured and assured tenancies 127
Assured tenancies 128
Other types of tenancy 128
'Common law' tenancies 129
Regulated tenancies 130

Agricultural tenancies 130
Crofting tenancies 131
What the landlord must include in a tenancy agreement 131
Changes to tenancy agreements 132
Preventing discrimination 132
Ending a Short assured tenancy 133
Other tenancy types 133
Ending a tenancy early 133
If tenants don't leave 134
If tenants want to leave 134
Ending a tenancy early 134
Houses in multiple occupation (HMOs) 134
Is the landlord a fit and proper person to hold a licence? 135
Is the property managed properly? 135
Does the property meet the required standards? 136
What are the landlord's responsibilities? 137
Tenants' responsibilities 138
Safeguarding Tenancy Deposits 139
Landlord's legal duties 140
Information about the schemes 140

Ch. 12-Relationship Breakdown and Housing Rights 141
Housing rights in an emergency 141
Approaching the council 142
Obtaining a court order 142
Long-term rights to the home 143
If you are not married or in a Civil Partnership 145

Tenants 145
Homeowners 145

Ch. 13-Housing Advice **147**
General advice 147
Government advice 147
Tenants Voice 147
Housing Advice Centres 148
Other specialist advice 149
Advice from solicitors 149
Free advice and help 150

Ch. 14-Agricultural Tenancies **151**
Farm Business Tenancies 151
Farm Business Tenancy rent reviews 152
Farm Business Tenancy compensation 152
Ending a Farm Business Tenancy 152
1986 Act agricultural tenancies 153
1986 Act Tenancies rent reviews 153
1986 Act Tenancies compensation 154
Dispute procedures 155
Contacts 156

Chapter 15-Mobile Homes and Houseboats **157**
Renting a mobile home 157
If you have a licence 157

If you have a tenancy 157
Eviction from a mobile home 158
Landlord harassment and illegal eviction 158
Repairs and conditions in mobile homes 158
Licensees 158
Tenants 158
Claiming benefits for a mobile home 159
Renting a houseboat 159
Housing benefit and universal credit 159
Paying council tax for a houseboat 160
Useful information on houseboats 160

Glossary of terms 161
Appendix 1-Useful addresses 165
Appendix 2-sample Assured shorthold tenancy agreement and notice 168
Index

INTRODUCTION

This latest edition of A Straightforward Guide to the Rights of the Private Tenant, **2025**, substantially updates the previous edition by introducing more detailed information concerning the law, landlords' obligations and tenants' rights and obligations. Given the crisis developing in the private rented sector, the situation is evolving quickly. The government is pushing the Renters Rights Bill 2024 through Parliament with the intention that it becomes law in the summer of 2025 (see below).

Information about private renting

Shelter offers many online resources, including housing advice. Contact a housing advisor. Citizens Advice also provides advice and guidance. The Tenants' Voice is the biggest tenant community in the UK and has a website full of information about renting and getting advice related to your rental problems.

www.thetenantsvoice.co.uk

General

More and more people, due to factors such as inability to access finance to purchase a house, are becoming reliant on the private sector. Demand is now exceeding supply, particularly in the major cities. Demand for housing in the private sector is rapidly expanding because of a combination of problems and rents are on the increase, in particular in London and the Southeast. In their recent report, Generation Rent, A Society Divided the Halifax states that the private rented sector is now at its highest level since the early 1990's. In 2025 there are approximately 4.4million households in England and Wales living in private accommodation.

With very little prospect of buying a home, more and more people will populate the private market over the coming few years. The response of the government to the rapid rise in private tenants and the corresponding problems of insecurity of tenure and sub-standard properties has been to tighten up the laws regulating the sector and also reduce tax reliefs for landlords to try to put a brake on growth and increase the numbers of properties to buy.

As a result, landlords are leaving the private sector, leading to a shortage of property to rent, particularly in the major cities.

In addition, the cost of living crisis that we have seen in the UK in the last 6 months, which has meant a rise in interest rates in an attempt to bring down inflation, has meant that rents are rising as costs for landlords increase. In London the situation has reached stupid proportions, with crazy rent levels and people, especially much needed key workers, are being driven out.

All in all, this is a perfect storm and a bit of a horror story and private tenants need to know, more than ever, what their rights are if they have a tenancy.

The Renters Rights Bill

The Labour government has announced its long-awaited plans to reform rental property management in England. The Renters Rights Bill, introduced in the King's Speech in July 2024, is Labour's version of the Renters (Reform) Bill that didn't pass through Parliament under the Conservative Government. This new legislation aims to enhance rights and protections for renters and is expected to be fully in force in the summer of 2025.

(It should be noted that all references to tenancy types and landlord and tenants' rights and obligations are framed within the law as it stands currently. These rights and obligations will change significantly following the passage of the above bill into law).

Main features of the Renters Rights Bill

- **Abolish section 21 evictions** and move to a simpler tenancy structure where all assured tenancies are periodic – providing more security for tenants and empowering them to challenge poor practice and unfair rent increases without fear of eviction. The government will implement this new system in one stage, giving all tenants security immediately.
- **Ensure possession grounds are fair to both parties**, giving tenants more security, while ensuring landlords can recover their property when reasonable. The bill introduces new safeguards for tenants, giving them more time to find a home if landlords evict to move in or sell, and ensuring unscrupulous landlords cannot misuse grounds.
- **Provide stronger protections against backdoor eviction** by ensuring tenants are able to appeal excessive above-market rents which are purely designed to force them out. As now, landlords will still be able to increase rents to market price

for their properties and an independent tribunal will make a judgement on this, if needed.

- **Introduce a new Private Rented Sector Landlord Ombudsman** that will provide quick, fair, impartial and binding resolution for tenants' complaints about their landlord. This will bring tenant-landlord complaint resolution on par with established redress practices for tenants in social housing and consumers of property agent services
- **Create a Private Rented Sector Database** to help landlords understand their legal obligations and demonstrate compliance (giving good landlords confidence in their position), alongside providing better information to tenants to make informed decisions when entering into a tenancy agreement. It will also support local councils – helping them target enforcement activity where it is needed most. Landlords will need to be registered on the database in order to use certain possession grounds.
- **Give tenants strengthened rights to request a pet in the property**, which the landlord must consider and cannot unreasonably refuse. To support this, landlords will be able to require pet insurance to cover any damage to their property
- **Apply the Decent Homes Standard to the private rented sector** to give renters safer, better value homes and remove the blight of poor-quality homes in local communities.
- **Apply 'Awaab's Law' to the sector**, setting clear legal expectations about the timeframes within which landlords in

the private rented sector must take action to make homes safe where they contain serious hazards.

- **Make it illegal for landlords and agents to discriminate against prospective tenants in receipt of benefits or with children** – helping to ensure everyone is treated fairly when looking for a place to live.
- **End the practice of rental bidding by prohibiting landlords and agents from asking for or accepting offers above the advertised rent**. Landlords and agents will be required to publish an asking rent for their property and it will be illegal to accept offers made above this rate.
- **Strengthen local authority enforcement** by expanding civil penalties, introducing a package of investigatory powers and bringing in a new requirement for local authorities to report on enforcement activity.
- **Strengthen rent repayment orders** by extending them to superior landlords, doubling the maximum penalty and ensuring repeat offenders have to repay the maximum amount.

Tenancy reform

The Renters' Rights Bill will introduce a transformative new tenancy system, ending the threat of arbitrary section 21 evictions, which uproot renters from their homes with little notice and minimal justification. The new tenancy system will provide tenants with greater security and stability and empower them to challenge bad practice without fear of retaliatory eviction. Landlords will also benefit, with more straightforward regulation, and clearer and expanded possession grounds.

Periodic tenancies

The Renters' Rights Bill will remove fixed term assured tenancies. Fixed-term tenancies mean renters are obliged to pay rent regardless of whether a property is up-to-standard, and they reduce flexibility to move in response to changing circumstances, for example after relationship breakdown, to take up a new job or when buying a first home.

Instead, all tenancies will be periodic, with tenants able to stay in their home until they decide to end the tenancy by giving 2 months' notice. This will end the injustice of tenants being trapped paying rent for substandard properties and offer more flexibility to both parties to respond to changing circumstances.

Grounds for possession

The government values the contribution made by responsible landlords who provide quality homes to their tenants and believe landlords must enjoy robust grounds for possession where there is good reason to take their property back. To support this, the bill clarifies and expands grounds for possession, while ensuring tenants are protected from arbitrary eviction and given enough time to find a new home.

Landlords must, as in the current system, go to court if a tenant does not leave. They will need to provide evidence that the ground is met. For mandatory grounds, the court must award possession if the ground is proven. For discretionary grounds, the court can consider whether eviction is reasonable, even when the ground is met.

Where a tenant is at fault, landlords can give notice using the relevant grounds at any point in the tenancy. This includes where a tenant commits antisocial behaviour, is damaging the property, or falls into significant arrears.

The government will introduce new protections for tenants who temporarily fall into rent arrears, supporting both parties by preventing tenancies which are otherwise viable from ending. They will increase the mandatory threshold for eviction from 2 to 3 months' arrears and increase the notice period from 2 weeks to 4. This will allow tenants more time to repay arrears and remain in their homes, while ensuring landlords do not face unsustainable costs. Landlords can also continue to use the discretionary rent arrears grounds, for example if rent is repeatedly late.

As well as tenants, landlords' own circumstances can sometimes change, and the bill includes strengthened rights to reclaim properties when it's necessary, for example to sell or move in. Tenants will benefit from a 12-month protected period at the beginning of a tenancy, during which landlords cannot evict them to move in or sell the property. Landlords will need to provide 4 months' notice when using these grounds, giving tenants more time to find a new home, and reducing the risk of homelessness.

In some sectors, it is necessary to move tenants on where accommodation is intended for a particular purpose, for example where the current tenant may no longer need the accommodation or is no longer eligible to occupy it. The government will therefore introduce a limited number of possession grounds to ensure there is an adequate supply of properties in vital sectors such as temporary and supported accommodation, and for critical housing schemes such as 'steppingstone' accommodation.

The government will also expand 'ground 6' for redevelopment to relevant social landlords to support redevelopment of properties where required and introduce a new possession ground for relevant social landlords where a tenant has been provided with alternative accommodation while redevelopment affecting the tenant's original home is carried out. Where the landlord seeks possession under these grounds, they will usually need to provide alternative accommodation that meets specific requirements.

To support compliance with requirements introduced elsewhere by the bill, the government will prevent landlords gaining possession if they have not properly protected a tenant's deposit or registered their property on the private rented sector database. The government will ensure landlords are always able to rectify non-compliance, so they are not prevented from regaining possession indefinitely. These restrictions will not apply to antisocial behaviour grounds.

Rent increases

The government will empower private rented sector tenants to challenge unreasonable rent increases. This will prevent unscrupulous landlords using rent increases as a backdoor means of eviction, while ensuring rents can be increased to reflect market rates.

In future, all rent increases in the private rented sector will be made using the same process. Landlords will be able to increase rents once per year to the market rate – the price that would be achieved if the property was newly advertised to let. To do this, they will need to serve a simple 'section 13' notice, setting out the new rent and giving at least 2 months' notice of it taking effect.

If a tenant believes the proposed rent increase exceeds market rate, they can then challenge this at the First-tier Tribunal, who will determine what the market rent should be. The government will reform how the Tribunal works to ensure tenants feel confident in challenging poor practice and enforcing their rights. Currently, tenants face the risk that the Tribunal may increase rent beyond what the landlord initially proposed – the government will end this, so tenants never pay more than what the landlord asked for. The government will also end the practice of backdating rent increases – with the new rent instead applying from the date of the Tribunal determination – to ensure tenants are not unexpectedly thrust into debt. And, in cases of undue hardship, the Tribunal will be given the power to defer rent increases by up to a further 2 months.

To ensure tenants always have a right of appeal, and prevent backdoor evictions, rent increases by any other means – such as rent review clauses – will not be permitted. This will also ensure all parties are clearer on their rights and responsibilities.

Implementation

To end the scourge of section 21 evictions as quickly as possible, the government will introduce the new tenancy for the private rented sector system in one stage. On this date the new tenancy system will apply to all private tenancies - existing tenancies will convert to the new system, and any new tenancies signed on or after this date will also be governed by the new rules. Existing fixed terms will be converted to periodic tenancies, and landlords will no longer be able to serve new section 21 or old-style section 8 notices to evict their tenants. This single date will prevent a confusing 2-tier system and give all tenants security immediately.

The government will work closely with all parts of the sector to ensure a smooth transition to the new system and will provide sufficient notice ahead of implementation. The bill makes specific provision to ensure a smooth transition and avoid unnecessary 'Cliff edges', for example maintaining the validity of rent increases and notices served prior to implementation.

The government remains committed to abolition of section 21 in the social rented sector too. While their intention is to do this as quickly as possible, they consider it necessary to update the Direction to the Regulator of Social Housing so that they can update their Tenancy Standard. This will ensure it is clear what registered providers must do under the new system. As this requires a statutory consultation process, the government will apply the new system to social tenancies (where the landlord is a private registered provider of social housing) at a later date.

Assured shorthold tenancies are typically only used in the social sector where there was an expectation that a tenancy would be for the short-term. As such, the majority of social tenants already enjoy secure assured tenancies, which have greater security and do not allow the use of section 21.

For more information concerning renters' rights in Scotland go to: scotland.shelter.org.uk:

For Northern Ireland, advice can be obtained from www.housingadviceni.org.

Powers of local authorities

It is important to understand the powers of local authorities when it comes to the regulation of residential accommodation.

Rogue Landlord Database, Banning Orders and Guidance Measures for Local Authorities to Tackle Substandard Practice

The previous conservative government released a range of new measures and guidance for local authorities that aim to tackle rogue landlords and letting agents in the private rental sector. The new measures come as part of the government's wider crackdown on substandard practice by landlords and letting agents, including a new database of rogue landlords and letting agents coming into force. Subsequently, local authorities have also been provided with a wider range of guidelines and powers on banning orders, civil penalties and rent repayment orders.

The new database will include landlords and letting agents convicted of a range of housing and immigration offences, alongside other measures including:

- Unlawful eviction
- Breach of gas & fire safety measures
- Leasing overcrowded properties

Local councils will also be able to share information concerning rogue landlords and the specific offences committed, allowing local authorities to keep track off or take further action with those who have a poor track record.

Banning orders for landlords and property agents

Working in tandem with the new rogue landlord database, the banning order for rogue landlords and property agents under the Housing and Planning Act 2016 has provided local authorities with powers to seek banning orders where the landlord or property agent has flouted their legal obligations or rented out substandard accommodation.

Civil Penalties under the Housing and Planning Act

The government has also published updated guidance on civil penalties, which aims to help local authorities use their powers on imposing civil penalties as an alternative to prosecution. The Housing and Planning Act 2016 gives local authorities powers to impose a civil penalty of up to £30,000 for a range of offences under the Housing and Planning Act 2004.

Rent Repayment Orders under the Housing and Planning Act

This extended guidance aims to help local authorities in using their powers to seek a rent repayment order against private sector landlords. The Housing and Planning Act 2016 extended rent repayment orders to cover illegal evictions and breaches of banning orders as well as a range of other offences. In addition to the above, there are new Acts banning tenants' fees and restricting deposits along with other measures, all covered in this book.

One case, outlined below, recently heard in the High Court is worth mentioning to demonstrate that Rent Repayment Orders really do have teeth.

Landlord to pay 95% of rent back after court rules home was 'unfit for human habitation'

A group of London renters have successfully managed to claim back 95% of their annual rent payments after taking their landlord to court. The property being rented out was an old converted bagel factory.

The judge ruled that the tenant's home, which was an old converted bagel factory, was "not fit for human habitation" The tenants living in the converted flat in Fulham, West London had to put up with water leaks, lack of fire escapes and doors, high chances of mold forming and concerns over asbestos in the roof.

The legal charity that supported the case, Justice for Tenants, www.justicefortenants.org said the lack of fire exits and doors in the property "caused great concern".

The group of renters and their landlord appeared at the First Tier Tribunal Property Chamber in London in February after having initially made their rent repayment order (RRO) application in June 2022. The tenants had been living in a warehouse that had been divided into eight units, with their part of the property having been "used to bake bagels".

The judge noted that there was "no evidence" that the landlord had got planning permission to change the use of the building to residential property. The judge ruled that the landlord had "acted in cynical disregard of his obligations as a landlord" finding "'no criticism of the conduct of the tenants". This was due to the landlord not providing any of the tenants with an EPC, a gas safety certificate, a record of the electrical inspections or the "How to Rent" checklist. The tenant's deposits were also not placed in a Rent Deposit Scheme.

Overall, the court ruled that the property was "prejudicial to [the tenant's] health as defined by the Environmental Protection Act 1990". The tenants received payments back on the rent ranging from just above £2,000 to just above £8,200.

Private Lettings and Selective licensing

Where selective licensing applies, unlike the other forms of licensing which relate to Housing in Multiple Occupation, (See chapter on Repairing obligations for more details on HMO's) then normally all houses within the private rented sector for that area must be licensed, except where they require to be licensed as HMOs. Non licensable HMOs must be licensed under Selective Licensing.

"House" means a building or part of a building consisting of one or more dwellings. For those purposes "dwelling" means a building or part of a building occupied or intended to be occupied as a separate dwelling

Designation for Selective Licensing

Selective licensing is dependent on a designation by the local authority. A local authority may designate the whole of their district or part of their district, subject to selective licensing. An area may be designated for selective licensing either (i) if the area is (or is likely to be) an area of low housing demand **or** (ii) the area is experiencing a significant and persistent problem caused by anti social behaviour and some or all the private sector landlords are failing to take action to combat the problem that it will be appropriate for them to take. A designation can last for five years. It can be renewed. There are prescribed publicity requirements for designations and the revocation of designations.

Properties to which Selective Licensing applies

Selective licenses are required for houses within the designated area where the whole of the house is occupied either under a single tenancy or license or under two or more tenancies or licenses in respect of different dwellings contained in it.

A tenancy or license is exempt from the selective licensing if it is granted by a registered social landlord.

The following tenancies/licenses are also exempt where:

- a prohibition order is in force

- business tenancies
- licensed premises (for liquor licensing purposes)
- agricultural tenancies
- the property is managed/controlled by a local housing authority or public body
- the building is regulated under other legislation (e.g. care homes)
- the building is occupied by students controlled/managed by a University/College (who subscribe to an Approved Code of Practice)
- the occupier is a Member of the family of the landlord/licensor who himself holds under a lease of the property for a minimum of 21 years
- holiday lets
- the occupier shares any amenity (i.e., a toilet bathroom kitchen or living room) with the landlord/licensor or a Member Of The Family of the landlord/licensor

Temporary exemptions

if the landlord is taking steps to change the situation so that the property will no longer need to be licensed.

Differences between Selective Licensing and HMO Licensing

- Generally, the same rules apply when granting a Selective License as with an HMO license. The main differences are: -

- It is mandatory to take up references for a prospective tenant before letting a property subject to Selective Licensing.
- Unlike HMOs the license authority does not have to consider suitability for letting or amenity standards when granting a selective license. However, the license holder must still be a fit and proper person.

Other legal developments for private tenants

Ghost landlords

A legal bid to protect tenants from so called "ghost landlords" has failed, in a move that could have significant implications for people looking to claim their rent back if they live in bad conditions.

In a landmark ruling the Supreme Court stated that a landlord is the person a tenant signs their contract with, and not the property's owner.

This typically happens when a secondary company offers guaranteed rent to property owners, they take the property on a lease and then become what is known as a ghost landlord. However, this has caused problems in that tenants are confused when they need to take action. Who do they take action against?

Housing campaigners say the ruling will be a "blueprint" for landlords to avoid taking responsibility for properties. But the National Residential Landlord's Association (NRLA) said it gives much needed clarity for those worried they could be responsible if secondary companies let out their home in poor conditions.

Those representing tenants and landlords say there has been an increase in a practice known as rent-to-rent which allows a company to rent a whole home from a landlord and then let rooms individually for profit. Critics say having a "ghost landlord" in this way often leaves properties in poor condition and tenants with nowhere to turn, and that some owners are using such companies to avoid legal repercussions. But some property owners say they too are being deceived by the same rogue operators and need the protection this ruling has given them.

Chain of tenancies

The court considered whether rent repayment orders for housing offences should be made against immediate landlords, or the "supreme landlord" when there is a chain of tenancies involved. It ruled that rent repayment orders can only be made against the immediate landlord.

The court said that rogue landlords can face other sanctions such as fines and banning orders and it is up to parliament to decide whether these are sufficient.

The NRLA, which intervened in the case in support of responsible landlords, said the case was never about whether legal obligations should be met, but about who should be held responsible in rent-to-rent cases. They said the ruling makes clear that rent-to-rent companies acting as a landlord need to make sure that relevant legal requirements are met.

"It is simply not right that such companies can take money from people without any responsibility for the property they are running," he said.

Rent-to-rent is not illegal, and those who promote it say it brings down rents by giving tenants the option of renting single rooms rather than whole house.

The overall aim of this book is to ensure that all are clear about the law and practice of letting and residing in, private sector tenanted property. The book covers the finding of property and the role of letting agents, detailed information on specific tenancies, payments of rent and benefits and repairing obligations. Issues such as unlawful eviction and harassment are covered, as are public sector tenancies plus tenancies in Scotland. There is a section on the processes involved in regaining possession of a home for breach of tenancy.

The various notices used when going to court, and other forms associated with landlord and tenant can be obtained from the county courts. All the necessary forms required in relation to housing matters can be downloaded from:

www.gov.uk/government/organisations/hm-courts-and-tribunals-servicebe The court service website also gives a lot of valuable information in relation to housing.

Finally, this book is relevant to England and Wales and also Scotland, although there are slight differences in Wales concerning tenancies. For example, every private landlord of a 'domestic tenancy' in Wales should be registered with the Rent Smart Wales scheme. This includes landlords of assured, assured short hold and regulated tenancies. In addition, landlords who self-manage those tenancies, or agents who have been appointed by the landlord, must have a license.

For further detailed information concerning Wales, Northern Ireland and Scotland go to:
sheltercymru.org.uk/get-advice/renting/private-tenants-rights/
For Northern Ireland shelterni.org/
Scotland scotland.shelter.org.uk

****

Ch. 1

Private Tenants-Looking for Property and The Use of Letting Agents

Letting Agents

One of the first places a prospective private tenant will look to rent a property is a lettings agent. It is important to know what the rules are governing agents as, particularly since the rise in demand for private properties, agents have started to use unscrupulous methods to extract more money from tenants and landlords, but particularly from tenants.

An amendment to the Enterprise and Regulatory Reform Act 2013 enabled the Government to require agents to sign up to a redress scheme. The Redress Scheme for Lettings Agency Work and Property Management Work (Requirement to Belong to a Scheme etc) (England) Order 2014 made membership of a scheme a legal requirement with effect from 1 October 2014.

The two approved schemes are The Property Ombudsman and The Property Redress Scheme. They will offer independent investigation of complaints about hidden fees or poor service. Where a complaint is upheld, tenants and leaseholders could receive compensation.

The contact details of these Schemes are as follows:

The Property Ombudsman Scheme 01722 333306
www.selfserve.tpos.co.uk
The Property Redress Scheme 0333 321 9418
www.portal.propertyredress.co.uk

The Government also amended the Consumer Rights Act 2015 to require letting agents to publish a full tariff of their fees. The charging of fees to tenants is now outlawed. Deposits are limited to five weeks, where annual rent is below £50,000 with new, stricter rules on holding deposits. The new rules (S.83 of the CRA) apply to all tenancies signed after 01 June 2019. Since April 2019 letting agents have been required by law to belong to an approved Client Money Protection (CMP) scheme to ensure that tenant and/or landlord money is protected should the business fail.

Online lettings agents

The rise of online lettings agents has been rapid and they now account for 3.5% of the market. The attractions are obvious, the costs. One such agent is www.openrent.co.uk another is www.onthemarket.com. Prospective private tenants can search sites for suitable properties. There are numerous online sites out there.

Responsibilities of lettings agents

Agents will typically transfer the utility bills and the council tax into the name of the tenant and sign agreements and take up references. They will sign an agreement with the tenant(s) subject to the pre-tenancy checks outlined below and go through the agreement pointing out such matters as whether pets are allowed or not. They will also, in most circumstances:

1. Organise repairs, although an agent will only normally do this if rent is paid directly to them and they can make appropriate deductions.
2. Chase rent arrears.
3. Serve notices of intent to seek possession if the landlord instructs them to do so. An agent cannot commence court proceedings except through a solicitor.
4. Visit the property at regular intervals and check that the tenants are not causing any damage.
5. Deal with neighbour complaints.
6. Deal with housing benefit departments if necessary. The extent to which agents do any or all of the above really depends on the caliber of the agent. It also depends on the type of agreement the landlord has with the agent.

Immigration Act 2014 and checking eligibility to rent

In October 2014, the Immigration Act 2014 came into force which puts the responsibility on landlords to vet their tenants, or prospective tenants to check to see if they have a right to be in the country (the obligation came into force in February 2016). Only when this is verified can a letting go ahead. In 2025, fresh updates were issued regarding all aspects of right to rent checks.

More information about the Right to Rent checks can be obtained from:

www.gov.uk/government/collections/landlords-immigration-right-to-rent-checks

Discrimination against tenants on housing benefits

There is a significant push to ensure that tenants on housing benefits are not discriminated against. From April 2019, Rightmove and Zoopla both took down listings that say NO DSS (the now defunct Department of Social Security). Others are likely to follow suit. Further, The Renters Rights Bill 2024 contains provisions that outlaw discrimination against people on benefits.

The letting process -Pre-tenancy checks

Before you can rent a property through a letting agent, you will need to show your passport or another document that demonstrates you have a right to rent in the UK. The landlord or letting agency want to be sure you will be a good tenant. There are various ways of doing this, and some are more flexible than others:

- You may be asked for references from current or previous landlords, employers, or someone else who can vouch that you will be a good tenant.
- You will probably be asked for evidence that you can afford the rent, e.g., benefit letters, pay slips/work contracts, bank statements (make sure you hide the account number).

- They will usually want to run a credit check. – Alternatively, you may be able to use a 'guarantor' – this is someone who signs to say they are willing to pay the rent if you do not and is usually a family member who will need to meet certain financial criteria themselves. You can find more detailed advice on the Citizens Advice website.

Payments at the start of the tenancy

You will generally need to pay your rent monthly and in advance. This means you will need to pay a month's rent upfront. At the start of the tenancy, you will also often need to pay the landlord a deposit (See below). This is to protect them against the risk of you damaging the property and/or leaving without paying the rent.

The landlord must put this in one of three government-backed 'tenancy deposit schemes' within 30 days. These schemes will make sure you get all your deposit back at the end of the tenancy, provided you keep to your side of the tenancy agreement.

It is possible that you will be able to get help with the payments at the start of a tenancy, through a rent deposit, bond and guarantee scheme run by a council, housing association or charity. Most of these are given to people who are homeless and/or 'vulnerable', so you will need to be in urgent housing need. You could check Crisis's Help to Rent database to see if there are any schemes in your area, though you will need to check with the local scheme to find out if you are eligible.

How to rent guide

As part of "The Assured Shorthold Tenancy Notices and Prescribed Requirements (England) Regulations 2015 "it is the law for your landlord (or letting agent) to hand you a copy of the How to rent guide at the start of the tenancy. This outlines what you and your landlord should expect from each other. It contains important information, such as: – questions to ask once you have found a property – how to navigate the ending of your tenancy – what to do if things go wrong.

Deposits-Tenancy Deposit Protection Scheme

The Tenancy Deposit Protection Scheme was introduced to protect all deposits paid to landlords (except landlords of common law tenancies such as company lets) after 6th April 2007. After this date, landlords and/or agents must use a government authorised scheme to protect deposits. The need for such a scheme has arisen because of the historical problem with deposits. Deposits are limited to five weeks rent, where annual rent is below £50,000 with new, stricter rules on holding deposits. The amount rises to six weeks for rents above £50,000. The new rules apply to all tenancies signed after 01 June 2019). The scheme works as below.

Moving into a property

At the beginning of a new tenancy agreement, the tenant will pay a deposit to the landlord or agent as usual. Within 14 days the landlord is required to give the tenant details of how the deposit is going to be protected including:

- the contact details of the tenancy deposit scheme
- the contact details of landlord or agent
- how to apply for the release of the deposit
- what to do if there is a dispute about the deposit

There are three tenancy deposit schemes that a landlord can opt for:
My Deposits
www.mydeposits.co.uk
info@mydeposits.co.uk

The Tenancy Deposit Scheme
www.tenancydepositscheme.com

The Deposit Protection Service
www.depositprotection.com

There are separate schemes for Scotland and Northern Ireland.

The schemes above fall into two categories, insurance based schemes and custodial schemes.

Custodial Scheme

- The tenant pays the deposit to the landlord
- The landlord pays the deposit into the scheme
- Within 14 days of receiving the deposit, the landlord must give the tenant prescribed information

- A the end of the tenancy, if the landlord and tenant have agreed how much of the deposit is to be returned, they will tell the scheme which returns the deposit, divided in the way agreed by the parties.
- If there is a dispute, the scheme will hold the disputed amount until the dispute resolution service or courts decide what is fair
- The interest accrued by deposits in the scheme will be used to pay for the running of the scheme and any surplus will be used to offer interest to the tenant, or landlord if the tenant isn't entitled to it.

Insurance based schemes

- The tenant pays the deposit to the landlord
- The landlord retains the deposit and pays a premium to the insurer (this is the key difference between the two schemes)
- Within 14 days of receiving a deposit the landlord must give the tenant prescribed information.
- At the end of the tenancy if the landlord and tenant agree how the deposit is to be divided or otherwise then the landlord will return the amount agreed
- If there is a dispute, the landlord must hand over the disputed amount to the scheme.
- If for any reason the landlord fails to comply, the insurance arrangements will ensure the return of the deposit to the tenant if they are entitled to it.

If a landlord or agent hasn't protected a deposit with one of the above then the tenant can apply to the local county court for an order for the landlord either to protect the deposit or repay it.

The Deregulation Act 2015

Since 6 April 2007, it has been mandatory for a landlord to ensure that a tenant's deposit that has been paid in respect of an assured short hold tenancy (AST) is protected within a Tenancy Deposit Scheme. The Deregulation Act now extends the requirement to protect a deposit to AST's created before 6 April 2007 in certain circumstances. Landlords are now required to protect their deposits within a scheme and serve the prescribed information relating to the deposit on the tenant. If a landlord fails to do this then it is prevented from recovering possession of the property from the tenant and is potentially liable for financial penalties.

Rental guarantees

The landlord is always advised to obtain a guarantor if there is any potential uncertainty as to payment of rent. One example is where the tenant is on benefits. The guarantor will be expected to assume responsibility for the rent if the tenant ceases to pay at any time during the term of the tenancy. More and more private tenants are having to provide a guarantor.

****

Chapter 2

General Information about Types of Lettings

In this chapter, we outline the differences between various property lettings and different platforms that can be used to obtain a property to rent. These are in addition to the mainstream flats and houses on offer.

Company lets

Where the tenant is a company rather than an individual, the tenancy agreement will be like an assured short hold but will not be bound by the six-month rule (see chapter eight for details of assured short hold tenancies). Company lets can be from any length of time, from a week to several years, or as long as you like.

The major difference between contracts and standard assured short hold agreements is that the contract will be tailored to individual needs, and the agreement is bound by the provisions of contract law. Company tenancies are bound by the provisions of contract law and not by the Housing Acts.

Short lets

Generally speaking, short lets are only applicable in large cities where there is a substantial shifting population. Business executives on temporary relocation, actors and others involved in television production or film work, contract workers and visiting academics are examples of people who might require a short let.

Short-let tenants provide useful extra income as well as keeping an eye on the place.

Short-let tenants are, usually, from a landlord's point of view, excellent blue-chip occupants. They are busy professionals, high earners, out all day and used to high standards. As the rent is paid by the company there is no worry for the landlord on this score either. A major plus of short lets is that they command between 20-50 percent more rent than the optimum market rent for that type of property.

The one downside of short lets is that no agency can guarantee permanent occupancy.

Student lets

In the past, many mainstream letting agencies did not consider students and a lot of landlords similarly were not keen. There was the perception that students will not look after a home and tend to live a lifestyle guaranteed to increase the wear and tear on a property. There has been a shift in this way of thinking and more mainstream landlords are letting to students. In addition, a number of specialist companies have grown up which concentrate solely on students. Although students quite often want property for only eight or nine months, agencies that deal with students make them sign for a whole year. Rent is guaranteed by confirmation that the student is a genuine student with references from parents, who act as guarantors.

Holiday lets

Before the Housing Act 1988 became law, many landlords advertised their properties as holiday lets to bypass the then rules regarding security of tenure. Strictly speaking, a holiday let is a property let for no more than a month to any one tenant. If the same tenant renews for another month, then the landlord is breaking the law. Nowadays, holiday lets must be just that; let for a genuine holiday. If you have a flat or cottage that you wish to let for holiday purposes, whether or not you live in it yourself for part of the year, you are entering into a quite different agreement with the tenant. Holiday lets are not covered by the Housing Act. The contract is finalised by exchange of letters with the tenant where they place a deposit and the owner confirms the booking. If the let is not for a genuine holiday, you may have problems in evicting the tenant.

Generally speaking, certain services must be provided for the let to be deemed a holiday let. Cleaning services and changes of bed linen are essential. The amount paid by the holidaymaker will usually include utilities but would exclude use of the telephone, fax machine etc.

Bedsits

Bedsitting rooms are usually difficult to let and can cause problems. There are numerous regulations to adhere to. Houses in Multiple Occupation regulations are quite strict.

The Housing Act 2004 introduced new tougher regulations for HMOs. If a landlord is letting out property in a block with more than three unrelated dwellings, then a license will be needed from the local authority before lettings can take place. (See chapter on repairs for more details about HMO's)

Landlords taking in a lodger

One way of finding accommodation is to approach people, through websites listed below, who wish to take in a lodger. the following are the main points to consider:

- Under the current Rent a Room Scheme a person can earn rental income of up to £7,500 a year (£625 a month from 2025/26) from a furnished room in their house, without having to pay tax on it. This is halved if letting jointly.
- Prospective Landlords can find lodgers using listings websites such as uk.easyroommate.com and mondaytofriday.com and spareroom.co.uk or fivenights.com (as their names suggest, the last two sites specialise in lodgers who need only weekday accommodation).
- A lodger may be a friend or relation; in other cases, it's important to vet anyone thoroughly before they move in. Experian, the credit reference agency, offers a tenants' screening service, under which a landlord can check a prospective tenant's identity, references and ability to pay the rent. The service costs from £15-£25. The prospective tenant must give permission for his or her details to be shared with you.

- A prospective landlord has certain responsibilities for example, they need to ensure that their gas appliances have been tested for safety. For more details go to gassaferegister.co.uk
- A prospective landlord may prefer to dispense with a legal agreement with the lodger but, if they prefer a more formal relationship, they can download the necessary documentation from lawpack.co.uk The agreement should set out every detail of how the arrangement will work, including rent, what parts of the house the lodger can use, whether guests can stay overnight, and on what basis the arrangement can be terminated.
- If the landlord shares their kitchen, bathroom or living room with a lodger, you can evict this person at any time – giving reasonable notice. This is normally 28 days. Under the law, the lodger is viewed as an "excluded occupier" rather than as a tenant. For more on this, see the government website: gov.uk/rent-room-in-your-home/the-rent-a-room-scheme.
- A prospective landlord should notify their home and contents insurer and their mortgage lender before taking in a lodger. If they are a tenant themselves, subletting a room in this way could give rise to problems: they should check their own tenancy agreement.

Letting through Airbnb

The Airbnb website enables people to let a room – or whole property – hotel-style, on an ad hoc basis. Landlords can charge considerably higher rates per night than they would charge a lodger, and there is greater flexibility as they may choose to let a room for only a few weeks a year. Airbnb hosts with stylish properties in London can charge £150-plus a night for a large bedroom with en suite, but guests expect standards commensurate with prices.

It is free to advertise rooms on airbnb.co.uk. The company sends a photographer to take pictures for your listing. Hosts use the Airbnb site's software to manage bookings, and they pay commission of 3per cent on each accepted reservation. Similar websites include Wimdu. However, Revenue & Customs could consider that regular hosts are running a business, so check before assuming that earnings qualify for the Rent a Room Scheme.

Kindroom

A new online platform called Kindroom, kindroom.com, is offering tenants accommodation in return for services. Kindroom brings homeowners and potential tenants together in a mutually beneficial relationship. Rather than tenants paying a hefty monthly sum for a room, tenants can move into a room either rent-free or at a low monthly cost in exchange for their skills and expertise.

Kindroom advertises homes to let, but in return expects tenants to offer "valuable knowledge in a field, expertise in a subject area or...a valuable skill or skill sets that can be exchanged for a space or a room to save money on accommodation." The platform allows tenants to browse homes, rooms and spaces in their desired location. They can then apply for the tenancy of their choosing, providing they match the required services of the host.

Kindroom requires hosts and tenants to register, similar to platforms like AirBnB and SpareRoom. Hosts can browse through the requests tenants have posted and select the tenants they feel match their needs. They can then communicate with the tenants before making a decision on one.

For example, one host is offering a free room in return for help with an ongoing court case while another is offering a free room in return for boxing, kickboxing and personal training sessions. Other hosts are looking for childcare and dog-walking, help to learn to drive, garden maintenance and someone with building/plumbing experience.

All these skills are in return for either a free room or a small monthly fee of around £200 - a drop in the ocean compared to average rental figures in the UK.

****

Ch. 3

Private Housing Issues for the Disabled

This chapter covers Disabled Housing in England. For housing rights and disabled in Wales, Scotland and Northern Ireland go to:

https://scotland.shelter.org.uk (Scotland)

https://www.housingadviceni.org/accessible-housing (Ireland)

https://sheltercymru.org.uk (Wales)

Generally

Despite the number of properties available to rent at any time, it can be challenging to find somewhere that meets your access requirements – or even to find out whether a property does or does not meet your access requirements. This is especially true if you need somewhere that is fully wheelchair accessible. Many private landlords and letting agencies advertise available properties online, using the rental pages of websites such as Zoopla and Rightmove. However, these websites don't currently allow you to search for accessible properties or particular access features. Rightmove can filter searches for bungalows, but these may or may not be fully accessible.

It can be a good idea to contact letting agencies that operate in the area you want to live in and explain your access requirements to them. You could search for an Association of Residential Lettings Agents (ARLA) Propertymark Protected letting agent. They may be able to identify potential properties for you and let you know as soon as they become available – though you may need to build this relationship and check in with them regularly. You should also be aware that letting agencies' loyalties ultimately lie with the landlord, so do not expect them to give you completely impartial advice.

Letting agents must by law make their application processes (e.g., any forms you need to complete) accessible to you.

There are also some companies that specialise in finding accessible properties –again, check that they are registered with ARLA (Association of Residential Landlords). In some areas, there are 'social' (not for profit) letting agencies and the criterion for using these agencies varies. For example, sometimes you need to be homeless and referred by the council –but it is worth finding out. Your council will be able to advise.

Making adaptations to a property

If you are finding it difficult to access basic facilities in your home or feel unsafe getting around your property, you may benefit from a home adaptation. Aids and adaptations are not only for people with reduced mobility; they may also help people with sensory impairments, dementia or mental health conditions. They could range from a small piece of equipment or technology right through to a major structural change, with the aim of improving your independence, confidence and privacy. If you live in a block of flats with some communal facilities, your landlord can make 'reasonable adjustments' to improve access to and within communal areas.

If equipment or an adaptation costs less than £1,000, your council (or in some cases the NHS) should provide this for free. You will need to get the permission of your landlord to make a change to your property, but, under the Equality Act 2010, they cannot refuse unless they have 'reasonable grounds' for doing so. Examples of things to look at to decide whether your landlord has a good reason for refusing an adaptation include:

- the type and length of the letting
- your ability to pay for the improvement
- how easy it is to make the adaptations (and how easy it would be to undo them)
- the extent of any disruption and effect on other occupiers
- If the adaptation costs more than £1,000, you will need to apply for a Disabled Facilities Grant (DFG) from your local housing authority. DFGs are generally means-tested but the council cannot refuse this solely because you are a private rented tenant, if you and your landlord are willing to confirm that you plan to stay in the property for the next five years. This is confirmed by the tenant and owner submitting a 'tenant's certificate' and an 'owner's certificate' respectively.

There are exceptions where the landlord can refuse to make the improvements, particularly if you are renting a room in a shared house, for example if: – the property you are renting has been the main home of the landlord – you share facilities such as the kitchen, bathroom or living room (the exception does not apply when you only share access to the property or storage areas) – the landlord or landlord's family member lives in the property, or – the property is not large enough to accommodate more than six lodgers or two separate households. At the moment, the Equality Act 2010 does not require the landlord to make structural changes to your property, or the 'common parts' of a block of flats.

Minor adaptations

'Minor adaptions' are changes that are made to the home and typically cost up to £1,000. Examples might include: – a short ramp and/or some grab rails – a door-release intercom system – changes to lighting and paintwork for a person with dementia and/or low vision. Minor adaptations can be approved and funded by your local authority, following an occupational therapy assessment, as part of a care assessment by adult social care services.

Major adaptations

Major adaptations typically cost over £1,000 and require substantial or structural works to your home. Examples might include: – the installation of a wet floor shower – ramped access that requires the widening of external doorways – replacing kitchen units with adjustable worktops – building an extension on to the property and/or a ground floor bathroom.

Funding and access

Disabled Facilities Grants can help cover the costs of major adaptations, whether you own your property or rent. The Grant is often means-tested based on your income, your partner's income (if applicable) and your savings, so you may well need to pay towards the cost of the work. The Grant is not means-tested if you are applying on behalf of a child under 18. Some local authorities have abandoned means-testing altogether. To start the process, you need to request an assessment for your social care team. Your local or district council is responsible for administering the Grant, which can provide up to £30,000 of funding. You can apply for funding to help with the costs of home adaptations whether you own your home or rent it from either a social or private landlord.

****

Ch. 4

Basic Elements of the Law in a Nutshell

Having discussed, generally, the access routes to private rented properties, and also issues for a disabled person, it is now very important to raise awareness of the law concerning property and rights and obligations under a tenancy agreement. Once you have signed a tenancy agreement, then you have a lot of protection under the law but also have a number of obligations.

Explaining the law

As a tenant, or potential tenant, it is very important to understand the rights and obligations of both you and your landlord, exactly what can and what cannot be done once the tenancy agreement has been signed and you have moved into the property.

Some landlords think they can do exactly as they please because the property belongs to them. Some tenants do not know any differently and therefore the landlord can, and often does, get away with breaking the law. However, there is a very strong legal framework governing the relationship between landlord and tenant and it is important that you have a grasp of the key principles of the law. This is particularly the case now the Renters Rights Bill 2024 is making its way through Parliament.

In order to fully understand the law, we should begin by looking at the main types of relationship between people and their homes.

The freehold and the lease

In law, there are two main types of ownership and occupation of property. These are: freehold and leasehold. These arrangements are very old indeed. In the section dealing with the relationship between leaseholder and freeholder, towards the end of this book, we will be discussing leasehold and freehold in more depth.

Freehold

If a person owns their property outright (usually with a mortgage) then they are a freeholder. The only claims to ownership over and above their own might be those of the building society or the bank, which lent them the money to buy the property. They will re-possess the property if the mortgage payments are not kept up with.

In certain situations, though, the local authority (council) for an area can affect a person's right to do what they please with their home even if they are a freeholder. This will occur when planning powers are exercised, for example, in order to prevent the carrying out of alterations without consent.

Leasehold

If a person lives in a property owned by someone else and has a written agreement allowing them to occupy the flat or house for a period i.e., giving them permission to live in that property, then they will, in the main, have a lease and either be a leaseholder or a tenant of a landlord. The main principle of a lease is that a person has been given permission by someone else to live in his or her property for a period of time. The person giving permission could be either the freeholder or another leaseholder. The tenancy agreement is one type of lease. If you have signed a tenancy agreement, then you will have been given permission by a person to live in their property for a period.

The position of the tenant

The tenant will usually have an agreement for a shorter period than the typical leaseholder. Whereas the leaseholder will, for example, have an agreement for ninety-nine years, the tenant will have an agreement, which either runs from week to week or month to month (periodic tenancy) or is for a fixed term, for example, six months or one year. These arrangements are the most common types of agreement between the private landlord and tenant. The agreement itself will state whether it is a fixed term or periodic tenancy. If an agreement has not been issued it will be assumed to be a fixed-term tenancy.

Both periodic and fixed term tenants will usually pay a sum of rent regularly to a landlord in return for permission to live in the property (more about rent and service charges later)

The tenancy agreement

The tenancy agreement is the usual arrangement under which one person will live in a property owned by another. Before a tenant moves into a property, he/she will have to sign a tenancy agreement drawn up by a landlord or landlord's agent.

A tenancy agreement is a contract between landlord and tenant. It is important to realize that when you sign a tenancy agreement, you have signed a contract with another person, which governs the way in which you will live in their property.

The contract

Typically, any tenancy agreement will show the name and address of the landlord and will state the names of the tenant(s). The type of tenancy agreement that is signed should be clearly indicated. This could be, for example, a Rent Act protected tenancy, an assured tenancy or an assured shorthold tenancy. In the main, in the private sector, the agreement will be an assured shorthold.

Date of commencement of tenancy and rent payable

The date the tenancy began and the duration (fixed term or periodic) plus the amount of rent payable should be clearly shown, along with who is responsible for any other charges, such as water rates, council tax etc., and a description of the property you are living in .In addition to the rent that must be paid there should be a clear indication of when a rent increase can be expected. This information is sometimes shown in other conditions of tenancy, which should be given to the tenant when they move into their home. The conditions of tenancy will set out landlords and tenants rights and obligations.

Services provided under the tenancy and service of notice

If services are provided, i.e., if a service charge is payable, this should be indicated in the agreement. The tenancy agreement should clearly indicate the address to which notices on the landlord can be served by the tenant, for example, because of repair problems or notice of leaving the property. The landlord has a legal requirement to indicate this.

Tenants' obligations

The tenancy agreement will either be a basic document with the above information or will be more comprehensive. Either way, there will be a section beginning "the tenant agrees." Here the tenant will agree to move into the property, pay rent, use the property as an only home, not cause a nuisance to others, take responsibility for certain internal repairs, not sublet the property, i.e., create another tenancy, and various other things depending on the property.

Landlords' obligations

There should also be another section "the landlord agrees". Here, the landlord is contracting with the tenant to allow quiet enjoyment of the property. The landlord's repairing responsibilities are also usually outlined.

Ending a tenancy

Finally, there should be a section entitled "ending the tenancy" which will outline the ways in which landlord and tenant can end the agreement. Currently, until the Renters Rights Bill 2024 becomes an Act, a landlord can only end a fixed term assured shorthold tenancy by issuing a s21 notice (so called because it arises out of section 21 of the Housing Act 1988, as amended) two months prior to the end of the tenancy.

The Deregulation Act 2015 states that the landlord cannot serve the notice until the tenant has been in occupation for at least four months. The tenant, after the expiry of the fixed term, can give one month's notice to leave. One more point worth noting is that, if the landlord issues notice, in the required format, by text or email this is likely to be accepted as valid notice.

The landlord must serve a notice by using Form 6A for all tenancies created on or after October 1st, 2015. This form must be used for all ASTs created on or after 1 October 2015 except for statutory periodic tenancies which have come into being on or after 1 October 2016.

If the tenants do not leave the property by the date specified on the form as the date after which possession is required, the landlord can apply to the court, within the period for which the notice remains valid, for a possession order using either the standard possession process or the accelerated possession process.

See appendix 2 for a sample Form 6A.

It is also in this section of the tenancy that the landlord should make reference to the "grounds for possession". Grounds for possession are circumstances where the landlord will apply to court for possession of his/her property. Some of these grounds relate to what is in the tenancy, i.e., the responsibility to pay rent and to not cause a nuisance. Other grounds do not relate to the contents of the tenancy directly, but more to the law governing that tenancy. The grounds for possession are very important, as they are used in any court case brought against the tenant. Unfortunately, they are not always indicated in the tenancy agreement. As they are so important, they are summarized later in the next chapter. However, once again, it should be noted that the grounds for possession will change with the passage of the Renters Rights Bill 2024.

It must be said at this point that many residential tenancies are very light on spelling out landlord's responsibilities. For example, repairing responsibilities are landlords' obligations under law. This book deals with these obligations, and also other important areas. However, many landlords will seek to use only the most basic document in order to conceal legal obligations.

This is one of the main reasons for this book. It is essential that those who intend to let property for profit are able to manage professionally and set high standards as a private landlord. This is because the sector has been beset by rogues in the past. Correspondingly, as a tenant you need to know your rights very clearly and need to know how to enforce them.

Key features of the Renters Rights Bill 2024

Abolition of Section 21

As mentioned in the introduction, the Bill, which is expected to become an Act in the summer of 2025, will remove Section 21 repossessions from the private rented sector. While this has been a central promise from the Labour government, it's worth noting that only about 6% of tenants face eviction through this method. Landlords will receive strengthened, clear grounds for possession to reclaim their properties when needed.

During the first 12 months of any new tenancy, landlords will not be allowed to move back into their property or attempt to sell it unless they sell to another landlord who will take over the tenancy. This means tenants will have a 12-month protected period; however, a tenant can serve notice to terminate during this period. Tenants will be required to give two months' notice to leave and this must be in line with the rent payment date.

Rent increases

An annual rent increase can be proposed by landlords. They must do this by serving the tenant a section 13 notice. Any proposed increase must be in line with local market rents and evidence provided if required. If the tenant accepts the proposed increase they will start paying from the next rent due date after the anniversary. *If a tenant believes the rent increase is above the market rate, they can dispute it by applying to the First Tier Tribunal.*

Abolition of rental bidding

Importantly, landlords and agents will be required to publish an asking rent for the property. This means they will not be allowed to encourage or accept bids above the stated price.

The responsibility of the landlord to provide a rent book

If the tenant is a weekly periodic tenant, the landlord must provide him/her with a rent book and commits a criminal offence if he/she does not do so. This is outlined in the Landlord and Tenant Act 1985 sections 4 - 7. Under this Act any tenant can ask in writing the name and address of the landlord. The landlord must reply within twenty-one days of asking.

As most tenancies nowadays are fixed term assured shortholds then it is not strictly necessary to provide a tenant with a rent book. However, for the purposes of efficiency, and your own records, it is always useful to have a rent book and sign it each time rent is collected, or a standing order is paid.

Overcrowding

It is important to understand, when signing a tenancy agreement, that it is not permitted to allow the premises to become overcrowded, i.e., to allow more people than was originally intended to live in the property. If a tenant does, then the landlord can take action to evict.

Different types of tenancy agreement

The protected tenancy - the meaning of the term

As a basic guide, if a person is a private tenant and signed their current agreement with a landlord before 15th January 1989 then they will, in most cases, be a protected tenant with all the rights relating to protection of tenure, which are considerable. Protection is provided under the 1977 Rent Act.

The assured shorthold tenancy - what it means

If the tenant entered into an agreement with a landlord after 15th January 1989, then they will, in most cases, be an assured tenant. In brief, there are various types of assured tenancy. The assured shorthold is usually a fixed term version of the assured tenancy and enables the landlord to recover their property after six months and to vary the rent after this time. *It is this tenancy that a private tenant will be signing.*

Again, it is worth noting that when the Renters Rights Bill becomes law the tenancy and the ground for possession will change.

Security of tenure: The ways in which a tenant can lose their home as an assured shorthold tenant

There are a number of circumstances called grounds (mandatory and discretionary) whereby a landlord can start a court action to evict a tenant. The following are the *mandatory* grounds (where the judge must give the landlord possession) and *discretionary* grounds (where the judge does not have to give the landlord possession) on which a court can order possession if the home is subject to an assured tenancy.

The mandatory grounds for possession of a property

There are eight mandatory grounds for possession, which, if proved, leave the court with no choice but to make an order for possession. It is very important that you understand these.

Ground One is used where the landlord has served a notice, no later than at the beginning of the tenancy, warning the tenant that this ground may be used against him/her.

This ground is used where the landlord wishes to recover the property as his or her principal (first and only) home or the spouse's (wife's or husbands) principal home. ***The ground is not available to a person who bought the premises for gain (profit) whilst they were occupied.***

Ground Two is available where the property is subject to a mortgage and if the landlord does not pay the mortgage, could lose the home.

Grounds Three and Four relate to holiday lettings.

Ground Five is a special one, applicable to ministers of religion.

Ground Six relates to the demolition or reconstruction of the property.

Ground Seven applies if a tenant dies and, in his will, leaves the tenancy to someone else: but the landlord must start proceedings against the new tenant within a year of the death if he wants to evict the new tenant.

Ground Eight concerns rent arrears. This ground applies if, both at the date of the serving of the notice seeking possession and at the date of the hearing of the action, the rent is at least 8 weeks in arrears. This is the main ground used by landlords when rent is not being paid. The landlord should understand that in order to get a court order for possession of property for rent arrears then, because of the short-term nature of the Assured shorthold, time is of the essence. If the tenancy is into the third month, it may be easier to wait and serve a two-month notice of termination and get a court order against the occupants separately. One of the advantages of a court order is that you will have details of the tenant's employers and can get an attachment of earnings against the tenant.

The discretionary grounds for possession of a property, which is let on an assured tenancy

As we have seen, the discretionary grounds for possession are those in relation to which the court has some powers over whether or not the landlord can evict. In other words, the final decision is left to the judge. Often the judge will prefer to grant a suspended order first unless the circumstances are dramatic.

Ground Nine applies when suitable alternative accommodation is available or will be when the possession order takes effect. As we have seen, if the landlord wishes to obtain possession of his or her property in order to use it for other purposes then suitable alternative accommodation has to be provided.

Ground Ten deals with rent arrears as does *Ground Eleven*. These grounds are distinct from the mandatory grounds, as there does not have to be a fixed arrear in terms of time scale, e.g., 8 weeks. The judge, therefore, has some choice as to whether or not to evict. In practice, this ground will not be relevant to managers of assured shorthold tenancies.

Ground Twelve concerns any broken obligation of the tenancy. As we have seen with the protected tenancy, there are a number of conditions of the tenancy agreement, such as the requirement not to racially or sexually harass a neighbor. Ground Twelve will be used if these conditions are broken.

Ground Thirteen deals with the deterioration of the dwelling because of a tenant's neglect. This relates to the structure of the property and is the same as for a protected tenancy. It puts the responsibility on the tenant to look after the premises.

Ground Fourteen concerns nuisance, annoyance and illegal or immoral use. This is where a tenant or anyone connected with the tenant has caused a nuisance to neighbors.

Ground 14A this ground deals with domestic violence.

Ground 15 concerns the condition of the furniture and tenant's neglect. As Ground thirteen puts some responsibility on the tenant to look after the structure of the building. Ground Fifteen makes the tenant responsible for the furniture and fittings.

Ground 16 covers former employees. The premises were let to a former tenant by a landlord seeking possession and the tenant has ceased to be in that employment.

Ground 17 is where a person or that person's agents makes a false or reckless statement and this has caused the landlord to grant the tenancy under false pretences.

The description of the grounds above is intended as a guide only. For a fuller description please refer to the 1988 Housing Act, section 7, Schedule two, as amended by the 1996 Housing Act) which is available at reference libraries.

As stated, there will be new grounds for possession of an assured shorthold tenancy following the passage of the Renters Rights Act 2024 scheduled for the summer of 2025. This follows a reappraisal of all grounds. For a full breakdown of the new grounds for possession and other changes go to:

www.gov.uk/government/publications/guide-to-the-renters-rights-bill/guide-to-the-renters-rights-bill.

****

Ch. 5

Joint Tenancies

Joint tenancies

Tenancy agreements

You have a joint tenancy if you and the other tenants all signed a single tenancy agreement with a landlord when you moved in. If each of you signed a separate agreement with the landlord, you have separate tenancies.

Right to rent

As we discussed, you can only become a private tenant if you have the right to rent. Each joint tenant must have the right to rent. A private landlord or letting agent must carry out a right to rent check before you sign up to a private tenancy.

Paying the rent when you're a joint tenant

Joint tenants are each jointly and individually responsible for paying the rent.

If one tenant moves out without giving notice or doesn't pay their share of the rent, the other joint tenants are responsible for paying it for them. If none of you pay your rent, your landlord can ask any one of you to pay the outstanding rent.

Tenancy deposits

The landlord normally takes a single deposit for the whole of the tenancy. Even if you and the other joint tenants paid separate or different shares to the landlord or agent. If one joint tenant fails to pay their share of the rent or if they cause damage to the property, the landlord is entitled to deduct the shortfall or the costs of the damage from the whole deposit.

You and the other joint tenants decide how to divide up the remaining deposit when it is returned.

Tenancy deposits when a joint tenant moves out

If you are replacing another tenant who is moving out, they may ask you to pay the deposit to them instead. This could cause problems. If the tenant who is moving out has caused any damage to the property or left any unpaid bills, the landlord can deduct these costs from the deposit when you move out. Get advice if you are in this situation. It might be better to ask the landlord to give a new tenancy agreement to you and the other tenants who are staying on.

How you can end a fixed-term joint tenancy

If you have a fixed-term tenancy (for example for 12 months) you can only end the tenancy before the fixed term ends if:

- you, the other tenants and your landlord all agree that the tenancy can end early (this is called a 'surrender')
- there is a 'break clause' in your tenancy agreement, which allows you to give notice and end your tenancy early
- You need the agreement of the other joint tenants to end your tenancy early.

How to end a joint tenancy that isn't a fixed term

If you don't have fixed-term tenancy or it has ended and not been renewed, you or any other joint tenant can end the tenancy by giving a valid notice to quit to the landlord. You can do this with or without the agreement of the other joint tenants. The tenancy ends for all the joint tenants. When the notice to quit expires none of you has the right to continue living there.

Leaving a joint tenancy

If you want to leave a joint tenancy and the others want to stay it is usually best to discuss it with the other joint tenants before you take any action.

If they don't want to move out, they can try to negotiate a new agreement with the landlord. The remaining tenants may be able to find another person to become a joint tenant with them. They must get the landlord's agreement for this. Or the remaining tenants could all agree to stay on and pay the rent between them.

However, if the joint tenancy has not been ended the landlord could still ask you to pay any arrears if the rent is not fully paid, even if you are no longer living there.

Eviction of joint tenants

Your landlord cannot evict one joint tenant without evicting all the others.

Your landlord may be able to end the tenancy and offer a new one to the remaining tenants. Talk to your landlord as soon as possible if you are in this situation and you want to stay.

.

Relationship breakdown

Your landlord could grant you a new tenancy in your name only if the joint tenancy with your ex-partner has been properly ended. You may also have other rights. For example:

- it may be possible for court to transfer the tenancy into your name – even if the other joint tenant won't agree to it.
- it may be possible to stop the other joint tenant from ending the tenancy by applying for an occupation order or an injunction.
- if you have experienced domestic violence, it may be possible to take legal action such as an injunction.

.

Problems with other joint tenants

If you have a problem with another joint tenant, you probably have to sort this out yourself. Landlords are usually reluctant to get involved, although council or housing associations are more likely to get involved than private landlords.

****

Ch. 6

The Payment of Rent and Other Charges

The payment of rent and other financial matters
If a tenancy is protected under the Rent Act 1977, as described earlier there is the right to apply to the Rent Officer for the setting of a fair rent for the property. However, given the effluxion of time, Rent Act Protected Tenancies have diminished to almost zero.

The assured shorthold tenant
It should be remembered that the provisions relating to private landlords and rent will change significantly with the passage of the Renters Rights Act. The outline blow deals with the law as it stands at the time of writing in April 2025.

The assured tenant has far fewer rights in relation to rent control than the protected tenant. The Housing Act 1988 allows a landlord to charge whatever he likes. There is no right to a fair or reasonable rent with an assured tenancy. If the tenancy is assured, then there will usually be a formula in the tenancy which will provide guidance for rent increases. If not, then the landlord can set what rent he or she likes within reason. If the amount is unreasonable then the tenant can refer the matter to the local Rent Assessment

Committee. The rent can sometimes be negotiated at the outset of the tenancy. This rent must be paid as long as the contractual term of the tenancy lasts. Once the contractual term has expired, the landlord is entitled to continue to charge the same rent.

On expiry of an assured shorthold the landlord is free to grant a new tenancy and set the rent to a level that is compatible with the market. Details of the local Rent Assessment Committee can be obtained from the Rent Officer Service at your local authority.

Local housing allowance (LHA) (housing benefit) for people who rent a home from a private landlord.

Local housing allowance is housing benefit for private sector tenants. It's usually paid directly to you and you pay your landlord. Local housing allowance is housing benefit that helps pay the rent and some service charges (if applicable) if you rent from a private landlord. It's a benefit administered by your local council. LHA has many of the same rules as housing benefit, but there are some extra rules that limit the amount of help you can get for a private rented home. LHA is usually paid direct to you rather than to your landlord.

Claim LHA

You can claim local housing allowance if you are a private tenant who needs help with paying the rent. You may be entitled to this housing benefit if you are working or if you claim benefits. Local Housing Allowance (LHA) is used to work out Housing Benefit for tenants who rent privately. How much you get is usually based on:

- where you live.
- your household size.
- your income - including benefits, pensions and savings (over £6,000).
- your circumstances.

Your LHA claim is routinely reassessed after 12 months. Your claim may be reassessed at any time if your circumstances change.

How LHA is calculated

The amount of LHA you can get depends on your income and savings and if any non-dependants live with you, for example adult children. The amount of LHA you receive also depends on the maximum rent allowed for properties in your area and the number of rooms the council decides you need. You can rent a home of any size or price, but your housing benefit claim is limited. You have to make up any rent shortfall.

Maximum LHA amounts

There are limits on the amount of LHA you can get. The maximum weekly LHA rate limits you are eligible for will depend on where you live. Local limits are based on the cheapest 30% of properties in an area. You should check with your local authority. for the current rates

Rooms allowed when calculating LHA

You are assessed as needing a bedroom for the following people in your home:

- an adult couple
- another person aged 16 or over
- any two children of the same sex up to the age of 16
- any two children regardless of sex under the age of 10
- any other child

An extra bedroom can be allowed if you:

- have a foster child or children.
- have a severely disabled child who needs their own room.
- or your partner are disabled and a carer provides regular overnight care.
- have a child who is away on duty with the armed forces and intends to return home.
- You cannot be allowed more than four bedrooms for the purposes of calculating your LHA.

If you're aged under 35

You are usually only entitled to LHA at the reduced shared accommodation rate if you are a single person under age 35 without children or you live in shared accommodation.

How often is housing benefit paid?

Payment of housing benefit depends on how often you pay rent. Housing benefit is not paid in advance. Each payment covers a previous period. Private landlords usually expect rent to be paid in advance, so you need to budget for this.

When LHA can be paid direct to landlords

Your council must make your LHA payments direct to your landlord if:

- you have rent arrears of eight weeks or more.
- deductions are being made from your benefits for rent arrears.
- In some cases, the council can choose to pay your LHA direct to your landlord. They could do this if you have failed to pay the rent in the past or you have problems paying your rent because of a medical condition. The council can pay LHA direct to your landlord if this will help you keep your tenancy.

If you have support needs, the council can pay LHA to your landlord to encourage them to keep you as a tenant. The council will consult you and people supporting you before deciding to pay LHA direct to your landlord. This may include your doctor, support worker, probation officer and others who know about your situation.

Council Tax Support

If you are in receipt of benefits, you may get help with your council tax through Council tax Support. Your local authority will advise you on this.

****

Ch. 7

The Right to Quiet Enjoyment of a Home

Earlier, we saw that when a tenancy agreement is signed, the landlord is contracting to give quiet enjoyment of the tenant's home. The right to quiet enjoyment is implied, if not explicitly stated within each tenancy agreement. It means that the tenant has a right to the undisturbed use and peaceful occupation and enjoyment of their home. Therefore, the landlord or freeholder cannot simply enter a property without giving either 'reasonable' notice or the amount specified in the tenancy agreement or lease that they intend to attend the property. This means that they have the right to live peacefully in the home without harassment.

The landlord is obliged not to do anything that will disturb the right to the quiet enjoyment of the home. The most serious breach of this right would be for the landlord to wrongfully evict a tenant.

Eviction: what can be done against unlawful eviction

It is a criminal offence for a landlord unlawfully to evict a residential occupier (whether or not a tenant!). The occupier has protection under the Protection from Eviction Act 1977 section 1(2). If the tenant or occupier is unlawfully evicted his/her first course should be to seek an injunction compelling the landlord to readmit him/her to the premises. It is an unfortunate fact, but many landlords will attempt to evict tenants forcefully. In doing so they break the law.

The Deregulation Act 2015 has introduced a new provision which deals with 'retaliatory evictions'. This is where the landlord has decided to issue a s21 notice on the tenant because they have complained about the landlord's service (for example repairs to the property) or unreasonable behaviour. If it can be proven that the notice was a 'retaliatory notice' then this will be invalid.

However, the landlord may, on termination of the tenancy, recover possession without a court order if the agreement was entered into after 15th January 1989 and it falls into one of the following six situations:

- The occupier shares any accommodation with the landlord and the landlord occupies the premises as his or her only or principal home.
- The occupier shares any of the accommodation with a member of the landlord's family, that person occupies the premises as their only or principal home, and the landlord occupies as his or her only or principal home premises in the same building.
- The tenancy or license was granted temporarily to an occupier who entered the premises as a trespasser.
- The tenancy or license gives the right to occupy for the purposes of a holiday.
- The tenancy or license is rent-free.
- The license relates to occupation of a hostel.

There is also a section in the 1977 Protection from Eviction Act which provides a defense for otherwise unlawful eviction and that is that the landlord may repossess if it is thought that the tenant no longer lives on the premises. It is important to note that, in order for such action to be seen as a crime under the 1977 Protection from Eviction Act, the intention of the landlord to evict must be proved. However, there is another offence, namely harassment, which also needs to be proved. Even if the landlord is not guilty of permanently depriving a tenant of their home, he/she could be guilty of harassment. Such actions as cutting off services, deliberately allowing the premises to fall into a state of disrepair, or even forcing unwanted sexual attentions, all constitute harassment and a breach of the right to *quiet enjoyment*.

The 1977 Protection from Eviction Act also prohibits the use of violence to gain entry to premises. Even in situations where the landlord has the right to gain entry without a court order it is an offence to use violence.

Remedies for unlawful eviction

There are two main remedies for unlawful eviction: damages and, as stated above, an injunction.

The injunction

An injunction is an order from the court requiring a person to do, or not to do something. In the case of eviction, the court can grant an injunction requiring the landlord to allow a tenant back into occupation of the premises. In the case of harassment an order can be made preventing the landlord from harassing the tenant. Failure to comply with an injunction is contempt of court and can result in a fine or imprisonment.

Damages

In some cases, the tenant can press for *financial compensation* following unlawful eviction. Financial compensation may have to be paid in cases where financial loss has occurred or in cases where personal hardship alone has occurred. The tenant can also press for *special damages,* which means that the tenant may recover the definable out-of-pocket expenses. These could be expenses arising as a result of having to stay in a hotel because of the eviction. Receipts must be kept in that case. There are also *general damages,* which can be awarded in compensation for stress, suffering and inconvenience.

A tenant may also seek *exemplary damages* where it can be proved that the landlord has disregarded the law deliberately with the intention of making a profit out of the displacement of the tenant.

****

Ch. 8

Repairs and Safety-Landlord/Tenant Obligations

Repairs and improvements generally: The landlord and tenants' obligations

Repairs are essential works to keep the property in good order. Improvements and alterations to the property, e.g., the installation of a shower. During the Pandemic landlords still had a legal obligation to carry out essential repairs and maintenance.

Most tenancies are periodic, i.e., week-to-week or month-to-month. If a tenancy falls into this category or is a fixed-term tenancy for less than seven years, and began after October 1961, then a landlord is legally responsible for most major repairs to the flat or house.

If a tenancy began after 15th January 1989, then, in addition to the above responsibility, the landlord is also responsible for repairs to common parts and service fittings.

The area of law dealing with the landlord and tenants repairing obligations is the 1985 Landlord and Tenant Act, section 11.

This section of the Act is known as a covenant and cannot be excluded by informal agreement between landlord and tenant. In other words, the landlord is legally responsible whether he or she likes it or not. Parties to a tenancy, however, may make an application to a court mutually to vary or exclude this section.

Standards of fitness

We have all seen the horror stories associated with mould recently, including the death of a young boy in Rochdale (see below AWAABS law). Although this was in social housing, the problem is prevalent in all sectors. Local authorities have a responsibility to determine that a property meets standards of fitness as described below.

AWAABS Law

The Government is set to introduce vital legislation in honour of two-year-old Awaab Ishak who tragically died following prolonged exposure to damp and mould. Landmark reforms to force landlords to fix dangerous homes or face the full force of the law will be introduced for the first time later this year (2025).

Initially, as part of the government's mission to transform the safety and quality of social housing, Awaab's Law will come into force from October 2025, ensuring social landlords must investigate and fix dangerous damp and mould within a set amount of time as well as repair all emergency hazards within 24 hours. Landlords who fail to comply face being taken to court, with social tenants able to use the full powers of the law to hold them to account.

It is intended that this law will extend to all private landlords in due course.

Implied standards of fitness for human habitation

The Housing Health and Safety rating System (HHSRS)

The Housing Health and Safety rating System, or HHSRS, is an official set of procedures for assessing health and safety risks in residential properties.

These procedures were introduced by the Housing Act 2004 and came into force in 2006, replacing the 'fitness for human habitation' rules of the Housing Act 1985.

What is a hazard?

The HHSRS identifies a total of 29 potential hazards that are associated with or arising from the issues outlined overleaf.

(See overleaf)

Damp/mould growth	Excess heat/cold	Fire
Asbestos	Crowding & space	Radiation
Biocides	Noise	Water supply
Volatile Organic Compounds	Lighting	Explosions
Food safety	Ergonomics	Entrapment
Hygiene	Intruders	Hot surfaces
Lead	Falls	Electricity
Carbon monoxide	Structural issues	Uncombusted fuel gas

What happens when a hazard is discovered?

When a hazard is identified in a property, two tests are applied:

- What is the likelihood of a dangerous event because of the hazard?
- If there is a dangerous event, what would be the likely outcome?

The likelihood and the severity of the outcome are combined to produce a 'hazard score'. Hazard scores are divided into 10 bands, with band A being the most serious and band J the least serious. Hazards in bands A – C are called Category 1 hazards and those in band D – J are Category 2 hazards.

If a Local Authority discovers a Category 1 hazard in a property, it has a mandatory duty to take the most appropriate course of action. If an authority discovers a Category 2 hazard, it has a discretionary power to act if this is considered appropriate.

Landlords who disagree with an assessment may appeal against it by first discussing it with the inspector and if necessary, challenging it at the Residential Property Tribunal.

Example of general repairs a landlord is responsible for:

- Leaking roofs and guttering.
- Rotting windows.
- Rising damp.
- Damp walls.
- Faulty electrical wiring.
- Dangerous ceilings and staircases.
- Faulty gas and water pipes.
- Broken water heaters and boilers.
- Broken lavatories, sinks or baths.

In shared housing the landlord must see that shared halls, stairways, kitchens and bathrooms are maintained and kept clean and lit.

Normally, tenants are responsible only for minor repairs, e.g., broken door handles, cupboard doors, etc. Tenants will also be responsible for decorations unless they have been damaged because of the landlord's failure to carry out repairs.

A landlord will be responsible for repairs only if the repair has been reported. It is therefore important to report repairs in writing and keep a copy. If the repair is not carried out, then action can be taken. Damages can also be claimed.

Compensation can be claimed, with the appropriate amount being the reduction in the value of the premises to the tenant caused by the landlord's failure to repair. If the tenant carries out the repairs, then the amount expended will represent the decrease in value.

The tenant does not have the right to withhold rent because of a breach of repairing covenant by the landlord. However, depending on the repair, the landlord will not have a very strong case in court if rent is withheld.

Reporting repairs to landlords

The tenant must tell the landlord or the person collecting the rent straight away when a repair needs doing. It is advisable that it is in writing, listing the repairs that need to be done. Once a tenant has reported a repair the landlord must do it within a reasonable period of time. What is reasonable will depend on the nature of the repair.

The tenants' rights whilst repairs are being carried out

The landlord must ensure that the repairs are done in an orderly and efficient way with minimum inconvenience to the tenant If the works are disruptive or if property or decorations are damaged the tenant can apply to the court for compensation or, if necessary, for an order to make the landlord behave reasonably. If the landlord genuinely needs the house empty to do the work, he/she can ask the tenant to vacate it and can if necessary, get a court order against the tenant. A written agreement should be drawn up making it clear that the tenant can move back in when the repairs are completed and stating what the arrangements for fuel charges and rent are.

Can the landlord put the rent up after doing repairs?
If there is a service charge for maintenance, the landlord may be able to pass on the cost of the work(s).

Tenants' rights to make improvements to a property
Unlike carrying out repairs the tenant will not normally have the right to insist that the landlord make actual alterations to the home. However, a tenant needs the following amenities and the law states that you should have:

- Bath or shower.
- Wash hand basin.
- Hot and cold water at each bath, basin or shower.
- An indoor toilet.

If these amenities do not exist, then the tenant can contact the council's Environmental Health Officer. An improvement notice can be served on the landlord ordering him to put the amenity in.

Disabled tenants
As discussed in Chapter Three, if a tenant is disabled, he/she may need special items of equipment in the accommodation. The local authority may help in providing and, occasionally, paying for these.

The tenant will need to obtain the permission of the landlord. If you require more information, then contact the social services department locally.

Houses in multiple occupation (HMO)

A landlord has extra legal responsibilities if the house or flat shared with other tenants is a house in multiple occupation (HMO). The extra rules are there to reduce the risk of fire and to make sure that people living in shared houses or flats have adequate facilities. From 1st October 2018, all landlords who fall within the HMO category must be licensed by the local authority for the area. A home is an HMO if:

- 3 or more unrelated people live there as at least 2 separate households – for example, 3 single people with their own rooms, or 2 couples each sharing a room the 3 or more people living there share basic amenities, such as a kitchen or bathroom. The requirement for the property to cover three or more stories of a property has now been removed and it is estimated that this change will mean that some 177,000 rental properties will now be classed as HMOs.

A home is a large HMO if both of the following apply:

- at least 5 tenants live there, forming more than 1 household.
- They share toilet, bathroom or kitchen facilities with other tenants.
- A household is either a single person or members of the same family who live together. A family includes people who are:
- married or living together - including people in same-sex relationships.
- relatives or half-relatives, for example grandparents, aunts, uncles, siblings
- stepparents and stepchildren

An HMO could be a:

- house split into separate bedsits.
- shared house or flat, where the sharers are not members of the same family.
- Hostel.
- bed-and-breakfast hotel that is not just for holidays.
- shared accommodation for students – although many halls of residence and other types of student accommodation owned by educational establishments are not classed as HMOs

Extra responsibilities of HMO landlords

Landlords of HMOs must make sure that:

- proper fire safety measures are in place, including working smoke alarms.
- annual gas safety checks are carried out
- electrics are checked every 5 years.
- the property is not overcrowded
- there are enough cooking and bathroom facilities for the number living there.
- communal areas and shared facilities are clean and in good repair.
- there are enough rubbish bins/bags.

Responsibility for repairs in HMOs

A landlord is responsible for any repairs to communal areas of A home. They are also responsible for repairs to:

- the structure and exterior of the house – including the walls, window frames and gutters.
- water and gas pipes.
- electrical wiring.
- basins, sinks, baths and toilets.
- fixed heaters (radiators) and water heaters.

HMOs don't need to be licensed if they are managed or owned by a housing association or co-operative, a council, a health service or a police or fire authority.

Licences usually last for 5 years but some councils grant them for shorter periods. When deciding whether to issue or renew a licence, the council checks that:

- the property meets an acceptable standard. For example, it looks at whether the property is large enough for the occupants and if it is well managed.
- the landlord is a 'fit and proper' person.
- Minimum bedroom size for HMOs.

If a landlord applied for a HMO licence on or after 1 October 2018 or has renewed it since, bedroom sizes must be at least:

6.51 square metres for an adult
10.22 square metres for two adults
4.64 square metres for a child under 10 years old

Some councils may set higher standards for bedroom sizes. If a room is used as bedroom and doesn't meet the size requirement, the council may allow a landlord up to 18 months to make the room larger or move you to a different bedroom. The council can prosecute or fine a landlord if a bedroom is smaller than standards allow.

Landlord penalties for not having an HMO licence

A landlord can be fined and ordered to repay up to 12 months' rent if tenants live in a HMO that should be licensed but isn't. A tenants can apply for a rent repayment order within a year of the HMO being unlicensed, and any housing benefit or universal credit tenants have used to help them pay rent will be reclaimed by the council.

Many people living in HMOs have an assured shorthold tenancy. If a tenant has an assured shorthold tenant and the HMO should be licensed but isn't, a landlord won't be able to evict tenants using a section 21 notice.

The council can prosecute landlords of HMOs, or any manager they have employed, if they break the law. In extreme cases, the council can take over the management of the property.

Safety generally for all landlords

Introduction to safety in rental property

Landlords are expected to consider the safety of their rental property and of their tenants and any other individuals visiting their rental property. Landlords do have a legal duty of care to their tenants. There are some very compelling reasons why landlords should make absolutely sure their rental properties are entirely safe.

Minimising risks in a rental property

Potential risk to tenants and their guests can be minimised by good property management practice. Landlords need to make regular checks of their rental property, looking out for any safety issues that arise; whether through wear and tear, any structural issues relating to the property, regulatory issues in terms of utilities or required servicing, or to do with tenant behaviour. Landlords should act promptly to fix any potential risks they pinpoint during these visits.

Accidents in rental property can lead to legal action

Accidents at a rental property can put a landlord into a whole lot of trouble. Any aspect of safety comes under criminal law – if a landlord is proven to being negligent to a general safety issue at a rental property, they could be put forward as having committed a criminal offence. Where found guilty a landlord could be faced with a jail term, a heavy fine, or both. In addition to any legal case a landlord could also face liability from the tenant for civil damages, and these can be substantial. The smallest injury can bring an expensive fine. Safety in rental property also extends to guests.

The issue also emphasises the importance of paying out for comprehensive landlord insurance cover. Don't skimp on a limited cover policy.

Items supplied in rental property

It is a criminal offence for a landlord to supply any item with a rental property that might be considered as unsafe. Some items such as oil heaters, portable LPG heaters, DIY tools, glass furniture and garden tools are particularly hazardous, and my advice to be landlords are best not to supplying any of these. They are all high risk and therefore best avoided.

Landlords should not forget to check the rental property before any new letting just in case any unsafe items have been left by a previous tenant. It these are defective it would be the landlord who is liable.

Landlords should pick up on any risks when they prepare a Property Inventory and Schedule of Condition. Any safety issues should then be either taken away or dealt with then.

It is important for landlords to remember that by providing an appliance or furniture that does not comply with the respective regulations may result in a criminal offence.

Following on from general safety, the main product safety regulations relevant to the lettings industry are:

Fire Safety Regulations in Rental Property

Following the Smoke and Carbon Monoxide Alarm (England) Regulations 2015 which came into force on the 1st of October 2015 all rental properties are covered by specific regulations concerning smoke and CO alarms.

HMO (House in Multiple Occupation) have additional safety and fire regulations to follow with the Fire Safety Order 2005 requiring landlord to perform certain duties including a Risk Assessment on their HMO in respect to fire safety.

Do landlords need to fit a smoke alarm in a rental property?

The Smoke and Carbon Monoxide Alarm (England) Regulations 2015 from the 1st October 2015 made it a requirement that landlords provide a smoke alarm on each story of their rental property and in certain circumstances, Carbon Monoxide Alarms are a mandatory requirement.

What are the smoke and carbon monoxide alarm requirements?

A rental property requires a minimum of one smoke alarm per floor, alongside this landlords and agents are required to have a Carbon Monoxide monitor in any living area where a fuel burning appliance is located.

What happens if Landlords don't comply?

If a landlord fails to comply with the new regulations, they could face a fine of up to £5,000, which falls to the local authority (Local Council) to enforce. As with all these regulations (well meaning as they often are) the complication comes in the detail and enforceability of the legislation.

What type of smoke alarm should I install?

The legislation is not prescriptive about what type of fire alarm or carbon monoxide alarm needs to be fitted. Prior to the new regulations properties built before 1992 landlords were allowed to install battery operated alarms. Residential buildings built or refurbished after 1992 were required to have a main wired smoke alarm. Smoke alarms can be brought online from as little as £6.50.

Who is responsible for testing and maintaining the fire alarms?

Landlords need to include a document possibly in their tenancy pack with the clear instruction that tenants need to test and be responsible for the replacement of any batteries required by the fire alarm. This instruction sheet should be included alongside the copy of the tenancy agreement, the property inventory and any appliance operating instructions, or emergency procedures information as part of a moving in pack given to tenants.

It is important for landlords have it determined who is responsible for the testing and maintaining the smoke alarms, whether the landlord, letting agent or tenant. If the letting agent is to be responsible, this should be noted in the management contract. If the tenant is to be made responsible for this then, adequate warnings must be given in writing by the landlord.

Fire Extinguishers in a Rental Property

There is no compulsory requirement for landlords to provide fire extinguishers or fire blankets in normal tenanted properties, but again, this may be a wise precaution by landlords, at least in the kitchen area.

If a landlord does make the commitment to provide fire extinguishers to a rental property, they need to be aware that they should arrange for a 12 monthly service of the equipment to make sure that they are not held responsible for any faults in the equipment. By providing a fire extinguisher it becomes their responsibility to have it regularly serviced.

Gas safety

The Gas safety (Installation and use) Regulations 1998
The Gas Cooking Appliances (safety) Regulations 1989
Heating Appliances (Fireguard) (safety) Regulations 1991
Gas Appliances (Safety) Regulations 1995

All the above are based on the fact that the supply of gas and the appliances in a dwelling are safe. A Gas Safety certificate is required to validate this. The gas engineer must be Gas Safe registered.

Furniture Safety

Regulations on Furniture and Furnishings in a Rental Property

From the 1st January 1997 all furniture in a rental property must comply with the 1993 amendments to the Furniture and Furnishings (Fire) (Safety) Regulations 1988. These safety regulations extend the scope of the Consumer Protection Act 1987 (CPA) to cover the supplying (hiring or lending) of specified goods (upholstered furniture and certain furnishings) "in the course of business".

The letting out of rental property is classified as 'business' and therefore the furniture and furnishings supplied by a landlord in a rental property come under these regulations.

The safety regulations apply to the following furniture provided in a rental property:

- Armchairs, three piece suites, sofas, sofa beds, futons and other convertible furniture.
- Beds, Bed bases and headboards, mattresses, divans and pillows.
- Nursery furniture.
- Garden furniture which could be used indoors.
- Loose, stretch and fitted covers for furniture, scatter cushions, seat pads and pillows.
- The furniture items excluded from the regulations are:
- Antique furniture or furniture manufactured before 1950.
- Bed clothes and duvets.
- Loose mattress covers.
- Pillowcases.
- Sleeping bags.
- Curtains.
- Carpets.

Compliance with the regulations on furniture

For furniture in a rental property to comply with the regulations they must carry a manufacturer's label which must be permanent and non-detachable.

- All upholstered items must have fire resistant filling material.
- All upholstered items must pass the "match resistance test" as prescribed.
- All upholstered items must also pass the "cigarette test" as prescribed.

- Bed bases and mattresses are not required to bear a permanent label, but compliance will be indicated if the item has a label stating that it meets BS7177

Summary of regulations relating to furniture supplied to a rental property

A landlord wanting to supply furniture must ensure that the types of furniture and furnishings listed above meet the current safety regulations. These regulations are enforced by local Trading Standards Officers. The reality is for most landlords these regulations are not an issue because they let their property unfurnished or part furnished, therefore without soft furnishings other than perhaps curtains, which are exempted from these regulations. For those landlords wanting to furnish a rental property the general advice is to furnish with new; given that it is an offence to sell non-complying items, anything new should be fine.

If a landlord does decide to use secondhand furniture, then be very careful. Here the correct labels are in place identifying the fact that the materials are fire resistant. will put tenants in a potentially hazardous position.

A landlord has a duty of care to the general safety of tenants and any other individuals visiting their rental property.

Electrical Safety

The Electrical Safety Standards in the Private Rented Sector (England) Regulations 2020.

Electrical Equipment (Safety) Regulations 1994

Plugs and Sockets etc. (Safety) Regulations 1994.

Electrical hazards are also covered by the Housing Health and safety Rating System under the Housing Act 2004. In the case of commercial property and houses in multiple occupation there is a statutory duty under the Regulatory Reform Fire Safety Order 2005 for the responsible person (the property manager) to carry out annual Fire Safety Risk Assessments, which include electrical safety risks.

The Electrical Equipment Regulations came into force in January 1995. Both sets of regulations relate to the supply of electrical equipment designed with a working voltage of between 50 and 1000 volts ac. (or between 75 and 1000 volts dc.) The regulations cover all the mains voltage household electrical goods including cookers, kettles, toasters, electric blankets, washing machines, immersion heaters etc. The regulations do not apply to items attached to land. This is generally considered to exclude the fixed wiring and built in appliances (e.g., central heating systems) from the regulations. Lettings agents and landlords should take the following action:

Essential: Check all electrical appliances in all managed properties on a regular fixed term basis. Remove unsafe items and keep a record of checks.

Recommended:

- Have appliances checked by a qualified electrical engineer.

- Avoid purchasing second hand electrical items.
- There is no specific requirement for regular testing under the regulations. However, it is recommended that a schedule of checks, say on an annual basis, is put in place.

For more information on electrical safety visit www.landlordzone.co.uk. This is a particularly good site.

From the 1st of June 2020 electrical installations need to be tested by a suitably qualified electrician who is a member of one of the accredited schemes for new tenancies and this will be expanded to existing tenancies from 1st April 2021.

Once tested, a copy of the up to date Electrical Safety Certificate or Electrical Installation Condition Report (ESCR) must be provided to both new and retained tenants.

The testing will be a PAT test which in case you are interested is short for Portable Appliance Testing and related to portable electrical items (not integral wiring systems) and include items such as: TV's, fridge freezers, kettles, etc.

If there is an issue with any of the electrical items tested than a landlord will have 28 days to address this.

Local Authorities will have a duty to enforce these new regulations and can issue fines of up to £30,000 where the landlord fails to comply.

Obligations on Landlords to upgrade and maintain insulation

From April 2018, properties rented out in the private rented sector are required to have a minimum energy performance rating of E.

The regulations apply to new lets and renewals of tenancies and apply to all existing tenancies from 1st April 2020. It is against the law to rent a property which has a rating lower than E unless there is an applicable exemption.

Buildings are scored for their energy efficiency, getting a rating of between A and G for the EPC system. A+ is the best score that a home can receive, showing that it can hold its heat better than other buildings.

At the end of 2025, new Government rules mean that any home rented out under a new contract needs to have a C rating or above. By 2028, all rentals have to be up to that level.

Private landlords face a big bill, as the data showed that nearly two-thirds (64 per cent) of private rentals do not live up to the standards.

The availability of grants

There are a number of grants available to landlords at any one time which will enable improvements to take place to a property. One of the main grants is the Disabled facilities Grant. However, there are more and your local authority can tell you what is available.

Legionnaire's disease

It is the responsibility of all landlords to undertake a risk assessment to prevent the spread of the Legionella bacteria, which can be found in a property's water systems and can lead to Legionnaires' disease if inhaled.

Legionnaires' disease is a pneumonia-like illness caused by Legionella bacteria and can be fatal. It is one of several conditions included within the Legionellosis group.

Although the risks are generally very low in residential property, health and safety legislation in the UK requires landlords to carry out risk assessments to control the exposure to tenants of Legionella.

The risk of Legionnaires' disease is likely to be higher in properties that are left empty and where water may be left to stand in both hot and cold systems, thus increasing the opportunity for the bacteria to multiply in the standing water.

As such, it is vital landlords ensure water systems are used at least once a week. And if a property is set to remain empty for several months, it may be worth draining the system to prevent the possibility of bacteria developing to unacceptable levels.

To minimise or eliminate the risk posed by Legionella, landlords should:

- Maintain cold water below 20 degrees C, as Legionella thrives in water between 20 and 45 degrees C
- Ensure showers and taps that are used infrequently - such as those in spare bedrooms - are periodically flushed through with running water
- Cover water tanks so mice, birds, insects and other creatures cannot gain access
- Remove unnecessary pipes, such as those leading to appliances that are no longer used

Signs of Legionella include cold water running warm, water that is discoloured or contains debris or a malfunctioning boiler or hot water system.

Sanitation health and hygiene generally

Local authorities have a duty to serve an owner with a notice requiring the provision of a WC when a property has insufficient sanitation, sanitation meaning toilet waste disposal.

They will also serve notice if it is thought that the existing sanitation is inadequate and is harmful to health or is a nuisance.

Local authorities have similar powers under various Public Health Acts to require owners to put right bad drains and sewers, also food storage facilities and vermin, plus the containing of disease.

The Environmental Health Department, if it considers the problem bad enough will serve a notice requiring the landlord to put the defect right. In certain cases the local authority can actually do the work and require the landlord to pay for it. This is called work in default.

****

Ch. 9

What Should Be Provided Under a Tenancy Agreement

Furniture

In the previous chapter we discussed furniture safety regulations. A landlord's decision whether or not to furnish property will depend on the sort of tenant that he/she is aiming to find. The actual legal distinction between furnished property and unfurnished property has faded into insignificance.

If a landlord does let a property as furnished, then the following would be the absolute minimum:

- Seating, such as sofa and armchair
- Cabinet or sideboard
- Kitchen tables and chairs
- Cooker and refrigerator
- Bedroom furniture

Even unfurnished lets, however, are expected to come complete with a basic standard of furniture, particularly carpets and kitchen goods. If the landlord does supply electrical equipment, then he or she is able to disclaim any repairing responsibility for it, but this must be mentioned in the tenancy agreement.

Insurance

Strictly speaking, there is no duty on either landlord or tenant to insure the property. However, as we saw in the previous chapter, it is highly advisable for the landlord to provide general and buildings insurance as he/she stands to lose a lot more in the event of fire or other disaster than the tenant. A landlord letting property for a first time would be well advised to consult his/ her insurance company before letting as there are different criteria to observe when a property is let and not to inform the company could invalidate the policy.

At the end of the tenancy

The tenancy agreement will normally spell out the obligations of the tenant at the end of the term. Essentially, the tenant will have an obligation to:

- have kept the interior clean and tidy and in a good state of repair and decoration.
- have not caused any damage.
- have replaced anything that they have broken.
- replace or pay for the repair of anything that they have damaged.
- pay for the laundering of the linen.
- pay for any other laundering.

- put anything that they have moved or removed back to how it was. Sometimes a tenancy agreement will include for the tenants paying for anything that is soiled at their own expense, although sensible wear and tear is allowed for.

The landlord will normally be able to recover any loss from the deposit that the tenant has given on entering the premises. However, sometimes, the tenants will withhold rent for the last month in order to recoup their deposit. This has become more difficult since the introduction of the tenancy deposit schemes described earlier. It is up to the landlord to negotiate re-imbursement for any damage caused, but this should be within reason. There is a remedy which can be pursued in the Small Claims court if the tenants refuse to pay but this is rarely successful.

A word on inventories

The Tenancy Deposit Scheme has released new guidance on inventory reports to support landlords and letting agents as a result of the Tenant Fees Act in June 2019.

Also known as the Tenant Fee Ban, the law – which applies to letting agents in England – means tenants cannot be charged for a number of extra services, including the provision of inventories. Landlords might then have to cover this cost themselves, rather than the charging or splitting costs with tenants. Without this option, some letting agents may choose to take the service in-house to minimise costs.

****

Ch. 10

Landlord Taking Possession of a Property

This chapter contains a general overview of the process of a landlord obtaining possession of a property. Given the nature of the problems which have grown in the private rented sector in the last few years and the increasing numbers of evictions now taking place (2025), it is of the utmost importance that tenants have a firm grasp of their rights. This chapter should be read in the light of the Renters Reform Bill 2024 which will abolish s21 notices and make it more difficult for landlords to recover possession.

To get a fully up to date overview of your housing rights when faced with eviction you should go to:

https://england.shelter.org.uk/housing_advice/eviction/harassment_by_a_private_landlord/understand_your_tenancy_rights

This is the website of Shelter and it has comprehensive advice concerning the process of eviction, covering everything from understanding your tenancy rights, how to check a notice (Form 6A) is correct when served and what to do if you are being forced to leave your property through harassment and understanding the powers of bailiffs. It also details the various advice agencies you can turn to if facing eviction.

Accelerated (Fast-track) possession

A landlord cannot serve a s21 notice (Form 6A) on an assured shorthold tenant until after the first four months of a tenancy (if it is for a six month period). This brings the tenancy to an end on the day of expiry, i.e., on the day of expiry of the six month period.

Rules for Section 21 notices

If the tenancy started or was renewed on or after 1 October 2015 a landlord will need to use the new prescribed Section 21 notice Form (6a). Form 6A has replaced both S21 and S8 Notices although the Form still relates to S21 and S6 of the Housing Act.

Section 21 (Form 6A) pre-requisites

A landlord cannot serve a valid Form 6A notice if:

- They have taken a deposit and not protected and/or served the prescribed information and/or
- They have failed to obtain a license for an HMO property which requires one

If the tenancy was in England and started or was renewed on or after 1 October 2015 a landlord must also have served on their tenant (and you should get proof of service for all these:

- an EPC
- a Gas Safety Certificate, and

- the latest version of the Government's "How to Rent" Guide.
- Which deposit scheme the tenants deposit is in

Plus, a landlord cannot serve a notice if their Local Authority has served one of 3 specified notices (the most important being an improvement notice) on them within the past six months in respect of the poor condition of the rental property.

Also, if the tenant complained about the issues covered by the notice prior to this – any Section 21 notice served since the complaint and before the Local Authority notice was served will also be invalid.

The notice period must not be less than two months and must not end before the end of the fixed term (if this has not ended at the time the landlord served their notice)

If this is a periodic tenancy where the period (rent payment period) is more than monthly (e.g., a quarterly or six-month periodic tenancy), then the notice period must be at least one full tenancy period.

The notice period does not have to end on a particular day in the month, as was required under the old rules – the landlord just needs to make sure that the notice period is sufficient – minimum of 2 months.

On expiry of the notice, if it is the landlord's intention to take possession of the property then the tenants should leave. The landlord should write a letter to the tenants one month before expiry reminding them that they should leave.

In the event of the tenant refusing to leave, the landlord has to then follow a process termed 'fast track possession'. This entails filling in the appropriate forms (N5B) that can be downloaded from Her Majesty's Court Service Website www.justice.gov.uk.

Assuming that a valid Form 6A notice has been served on the tenant, the accelerated possession proceedings can begin and the forms completed and lodged with the court dealing with the area where the property is situated. In order to grant the accelerated possession order the court will require the following:

- The assured shorthold agreement
- The section 21 notice (Form 6A)
- Evidence of service of the notice

If a landlord has already served the notice, then evidence that the tenant has received it will be required. Having the correct original paperwork is of the utmost importance. Without this, the application will fail and delays will be incurred.

If the tenant disputes the possession proceedings in any way, they will have 14 days to reply to the court. Once the accelerated possession order has been granted then this will need to be served on the tenant, giving them 14 days to vacate. In certain circumstances, if the tenant pleads hardship the court can grant extra time to leave, six weeks as opposed to two weeks. If they still do not vacate, then an application will need to be made to court for a bailiff's warrant to evict the tenants.

Accelerated possession proceedings cannot be used against the tenant for rent arrears. It will be necessary to follow the procedure below.

An accelerated possession order remains in force for six years from the date it was granted.

Going to court to end the tenancy

There may come a time when a landlord needs to go to court to regain possession of their property. This will usually arise when the contract has been breached by the tenant, for non-payment of rent or for some other breach such as nuisance or harassment. As we have seen, a tenancy can be ended in a court on one of the grounds for possession. However, as the tenancy will usually be an assured shorthold then it is necessary for the landlord to consider whether they are in a position to give two months notice and withhold the deposit, as opposed to going to court. The act of withholding the deposit will entail the landlord refusing to authorize the payment to the tenant online. This then brings arbitration into the frame. Deposit schemes have an arbitration system as an integral part of the scheme.

If a landlord decides, for whatever reason, to go to court, then any move to regain a property for breach of agreement will commence in the county court in the area in which the property is. The first steps in ending the tenancy will necessitate the serving of a notice of seeking possession Form 6A using one of the Grounds for Possession detailed earlier in the book. If the tenancy is protected then 28 days must be given, the notice must be in prescribed form and served on the tenant personally (preferably).

If the tenancy is an assured shorthold, which is usually the case then 14 days' notice of seeking possession can be used. In all cases the ground to be relied upon must be clearly outlined in the notice. If the case is more complex, then this will entail a particulars of claim being prepared, usually by a solicitor, as opposed to a standard possession form.

A fee is paid when sending the particulars to court, which should be checked with the local county court. The standard form which the landlord uses for routine rent arrears cases is called the N119 and the accompanying summons is called the N5. Both forms can be obtained from the court or from www.courtservice.gov. When completed, the forms are sent in duplicate to the county court and a copy retained for the landlord.

The court will send a copy of the particulars of claim and the summons to the tenant. They will send the landlord a form which gives them a case number and court date to appear, known as the return date. On the return date, the landlord should arrive at court at least 15 minutes early. Complainants can represent themselves in simple cases but are advised to use a solicitor for more contentious cases.

If the tenant is present, then they will have a chance to defend themselves.

A number of orders are available. However, if a landlord has gone to court on the mandatory ground eight then if the fact is proved then they will get possession immediately. If not, then the judge can grant an order, suspended whilst the tenant finds time to pay.

In a lot of cases, it is more expedient for a landlord to serve notice-requiring possession, if the tenancy has reached the end of the period and then wait two months before the property is regained. This saves the cost and time of going to court particularly if the ground is one of nuisance or other, which will involve solicitors.

In many cases, if landlords are contemplating going to court and have never been before and do not know the procedure then it is best to use a solicitor to guide the case through.

Costs can be recovered from the tenant, although this will depend on their means. If possession is regained midway through the contractual term, then the landlord will have to complete the possession process by use of bailiff, pay a fee and fill in another form, Warrant for Possession of Land.

If a landlord has reached the end of the contractual term and wish to recover their property, then a fast track procedure is available which entails gaining an order for possession and bailiff's order by post. This can be used in cases except for rent arrears.

Ending your tenancy legally

Make sure you end your tenancy legally if you're willing to move out. Write to your landlord by post or email. Be clear about when you want the tenancy to end. You're responsible for rent until the tenancy ends, even if you move out earlier. Your landlord should be flexible if they want you to leave without court action.

Giving notice to your landlord

If you cannot agree on a tenancy end date, you can usually end your tenancy by giving notice. Your landlord can evict you without a court order if you give them a valid notice. Only give notice under a break clause or notice to quit if you're sure you can leave by the date in the notice.

Agreeing to end the tenancy

Some landlords suggest ending the tenancy by agreement instead of eviction through the courts. This is sometimes called a 'mutual surrender'. Although a tenancy surrender can save you court costs it is unlikely to be a good option until you have found somewhere else to live. Do not sign anything that could end your right to live in your home if you have nowhere else to go.

****

Ch. 11

Private Tenancies in Scotland

Scotland rent freeze and eviction ban 2023

Changes to rent controls in Scotland

Temporary restrictions on rent increases were introduced in 2022 to address the cost-of-living crisis, but these measures have now been withdrawn.

Scottish rent controls expired on March 31, 2025, allowing landlords to set rents without restrictions until the Housing (Scotland) Bill comes into effect in 2027.

The Housing Bill (Scotland) 2024

The Housing (Scotland) Bill is a Scottish Government Bill introduced in the Parliament on 26 March 2024. The Bill deals mainly with rented, particularly private rented, accommodation and homelessness prevention. The Scottish Government states that the package of reforms, "will help ensure people have a safe, secure, and affordable place to live .... while contributing to the ambition to end homelessness in Scotland."

Part 1 relates to rent paid by private tenants. It includes:

• duties on local authorities to assess rent conditions in their area, at least once every five years.

• powers for Scottish Ministers to designate rent control areas. In rent control areas, rent increases would be restricted for existing and new tenancies with some exceptions made for new to market properties.
• limits on how often rent can increase during a tenancy both in and outside of rent control areas.
• powers for local authorities to gather information on rents and other information about properties on the private landlord register.

Part 2 of the Bill deals with evictions. It places a duty on the First-tier Tribunal for Scotland and the courts to consider whether to delay when an eviction can be carried out.
It also changes how damages for unlawful eviction are calculated.

Part 3 introduces new rights:
• for private and social housing tenants to request to keep a pet • for private housing tenants to make changes to the property they are renting.

Part 4 makes changes to other matters affecting tenants, including:
• allowing unclaimed tenancy deposits to be used to provide support to private tenants across Scotland
• changing how a joint private residential tenancy can be ended by allowing a single joint tenant to end a joint tenancy after giving notice to the other tenant(s)
• giving Scottish Ministers the power to convert assured tenancies into private residential tenancies.

Part 5 of the Bill relates to homelessness prevention. Proposed changes include:

• placing duties on relevant bodies, such as health boards or the police, to ask if an individual is homeless or at risk of homelessness, and requires them to take action if they are - the aim being to make homelessness prevention a shared responsibility across the public sector

• requiring local authorities act sooner to prevent homelessness by providing support to households threatened with homelessness up to 6 months before homelessness appears imminent rather than the current 2 months

• making social landlords put in place support for tenants if they are overdue on rent due to domestic abuse • requiring social landlords to have a policy which sets out how they will support tenants who are at risk of homelessness due to domestic abuse.

Part 6 deals with other housing matters including:

• changing the way mobile home pitch fees are presumed to be calculated so increases follow the Consumer Prices Index (CPI) rather than the Retail Prices Index (RPI)

• changing the reporting and consultation requirements in the Fuel Poverty (Targets, Definition and Strategy) (Scotland) Act 2019 and removing some limits on the operating costs of the Scottish Fuel Poverty Advisory Panel

• allowing the Scottish Public Services Ombudsman (who investigates, reports on and helps settle complaints) to share information with the New Homes Ombudsman for the UK.

The 2024 Bill is making its way through the Scottish Parliament and is set to become law sometime in 2025. The situation as it stands is dealt with below.

The law generally in Scotland

The law governing the relationship between private landlords and tenants in Scotland is different to that in England. Since the beginning of 1989, new private sector tenancies in Scotland were covered by the Housing (Scotland) Act 1988. Following the passage of this Act, private sector tenants no longer had any protection as far as rent levels were concerned and tenants enjoyed less security of tenure. However, **The Private Housing (Tenancies) (Scotland) Act 2016**, passed by the Scottish Parliament which came into force on 1st December 2017 changed the law concerning private tenancies in Scotland. The main provisions of the Act are outlined below.

The Private Residential Tenancy-Scotland

On 1 December 2017 a new type of tenancy came into force, called the private residential tenancy, it replaced assured and short assured tenancy agreements for all new tenancies from 1st December 2017, as a result of the passing of The Private Housing (Tenancies) (Scotland) Act 2016. The new Scottish Private Residential Tenancy, (SPRT) will deliver improved security of tenure for tenants, including students in smaller purpose built and mainstream private rented accommodation, and also the power for local authorities to designate rent pressure zones within their jurisdiction. There will also be streamlined procedures for starting and ending a tenancy and a model agreement for landlords and tenants.

The SPRT will become the standard tenancy agreement between residential landlords and tenants and will replace the most common types of residential tenancies in Scotland – the Short Assured Tenancy and the Assured Tenancy.

Any tenancy that started on or after 1 December 2017 will be a private residential tenancy. These new tenancies will bring in changes and improvements to the private rented sector, including:

- **No more fixed terms** - private residential tenancies are open ended, meaning a landlord can't ask a tenant to leave just because they have been in the property for 6 months as they can with a short assured tenancy.
- **Rent increases** – a tenant's rent can only be increased once every 12 months (with 3 months' notice) and if they think the proposed increase is unfair, they can refer it to a rent officer. (Consider the rules governing the current rent freeze)
- **Longer notice period** - if a tenant has lived in a property for longer than 6 months the landlord will have to give them at least 84 days notice to leave (unless they have broken a term in the tenancy).
- **Simpler notices** - the notice to quit process has been scrapped and replaced by a simpler notice to leave process.
- **Model tenancy agreement** - the Scottish Government have published a model private residential tenancy that can be used by landlords to set up a tenancy.

Person already an assured/short assured tenant

If a tenant was already renting and were an assured or short assured tenant, on 1 December 2017, their tenancy will continue as normal until they or their landlord brings it to an end following the correct procedure. If a landlord then offers a tenant a new tenancy this will be a private residential tenancy.

What is a private residential tenancy?

A private residential tenancy is one that meets the following conditions:

- the tenancy started on or after 1 December 2017
- it is let to a person as a separate dwelling (home)
- the person must be an individual, meaning not a company
- it's their main or only home
- they must have a lease (although a written agreement not needed for a lease to exist)
- the tenancy is not a exemptions tenancy, as listed below.

Tenancy agreements

A person has the right to a tenancy agreement, which can be either a written or electronic copy, within 28 days of the start of the tenancy. The Scottish Government has published a model tenancy that a landlord can use to set up a tenancy. This tenancy plus a set of notes that a landlord must give to the tenant can be accessed at www.mygov.scot/tenancy-agreement-scotland.

This tenancy agreement contains certain statutory terms that outline both party's rights and obligations including:

- The tenant's and landlord/letting agent's contact details
- The address and details of the rented property
- The start date of the tenancy
- How much the rent is and how it can be increased
- How much the deposit is and information about how it will be registered
- Who is responsible for insuring the property
- The tenant has to inform the landlord when they are going to be absent from the property for more than 14 days
- The tenant will take reasonable care of the property
- The condition that the landlord must make sure the property is in, including the repairing standard.
- That the tenant must inform the landlord the need of any repairs.
- That the tenant will give reasonable access to the property, when the landlord has given at least 48 hours notice

The process through which a tenancy can be brought to an end

If a landlord uses the Scottish Government's' model tenancy, they should also give the tenant the 'Easy Read Notes' which will explain the tenancy terms in plain English.

If a landlord does not use the model tenancy, they must give the tenant the private residential tenancy statutory terms: supporting notes, with their lease, which will explains the basic set of terms that a landlord has to include in the lease.

Ending a tenancy

If a tenant wants to end the tenancy, then they will have to give the landlord 28 days' notice in writing. The notice must state the day on which the tenancy is to end, normally the day after the notice period has expired. The tenant can agree a different notice period with the landlord as long it is in writing. If there is no agreed notice, then 28 days' notice is the minimum required.

Landlord access

The tenant must allow reasonable access to the landlord to carry out repairs, inspections, or valuations when:

- the landlord has given at least 48 hours' written notice, or
- access is required urgently for the landlord to view or carry out works in relation to the repairing standard

If a tenant refuses access the landlord can make an application to the First Tier Tribunal Housing and Property Chamber who may make an order allowing them access.

Getting repairs carried out

As with other tenancies, the landlord must keep the property wind and watertight, and in a condition that is safe to live in. The landlord is also responsible for making sure that the property repairing standard is met. This is a basic level of repair that is required by law. The landlord must give the tenant information on the repairing standard and what they can do if the property does not meet it.

If a tenant wants to carry out work on their home, such as redecorating or installing a second phone line, they will need to seek permission from the landlord. Some tenancy agreements will include a clause telling the tenant whether they can carry out this kind of work.

Can a tenant sublet or pass their tenancy on to someone else?
A tenant cannot sublet, take in a lodger or pass their tenancy on to someone else before first getting written agreement from the landlord.

Tenancies that cannot be a private residential tenancy
Almost all new private tenancies created on or after 1st December 2017 will be private residential tenancies.

However, there are a number of exemptions, including the following:

- Tenancies at a low rent
- Tenancies of shops
- Licensed premises
- Tenancies of agricultural land
- Lettings to students (meaning purpose built student accommodation)
- Holiday lettings
- Resident landlords
- Police Housing

- Military Housing
- Social Housing
- Sublet, assigned etc. social housing
- Homeless persons
- Persons on probation or released from prison etc.
- Accommodation for asylum seekers
- Displaced persons
- Shared ownership
- Tenancies under previous legislation
- Assured or short assured tenancies

Short assured and assured tenancies

Most residential lettings in Scotland made after 2 January 1989 and before 1st December 2017 are short assured tenancies. Those that aren't short assured are normally assured tenancies.

Short assured tenancies

This was the most common type of tenancy. A short assured tenancy makes it easier for a landlord to get a property than an assured tenancy. Before any agreement is signed, a landlord must use form AT5 to tell new tenants that the tenancy will be a short assured tenancy. If they don't, the tenancy will automatically be an assured tenancy. Initially, a short assured tenancy must be for 6 months or more. After the first 6 months, the tenancy can be renewed for a shorter period.

Assured tenancies

At the beginning of an assured tenancy, it will be classed as a 'contractual assured tenancy' for a fixed period. The tenancy automatically becomes a 'statutory assured tenancy' if:

- the landlord ends the tenancy by issuing a notice to quit (e.g., because they want to change the agreement) and the tenant stays in the property
- the fixed period covered by the tenancy comes to an end and the tenant stays in the property

There are different rights and responsibilities on both landlord and tenant depending on the type of assured tenancy.

Other types of tenancy

Most tenancies in Scotland issued before December 2017 are short assured or assured tenancies.

The other tenancy types are:

- 'common law' tenancy - if a tenant shares their home as a lodger
- regulated tenancy - the most common form of tenancy before 1989
- agricultural tenancy
- crofting tenancy

'Common law' tenancies

If a landlord is sharing their house or flat with their tenants, they can't use the short assured or assured tenancy. Instead, they will automatically have what is known as a 'common law tenancy'. The tenant doesn't have to have a written contract, but the landlord may use a lodger agreement to create a contract between them and the tenant - so both are clear about what has been agreed.

Regulated tenancies

Tenancies created before 2 January 1989 are generally regulated tenancies. As not many exist we will not be describing them further here.

Agricultural tenancies

There are 3 types of agricultural tenancy:

- limited duration tenancy - if the lease is for more than 5 years
- short limited duration tenancy - if the lease is for 5 years or less
- 1991 Act tenancy - if the tenancy began before 2003

All agricultural tenants have the right to:

- a written lease
- compensation at the end of the tenancy for any improvements they made to the land during their tenancy
- leave the tenancy to a spouse or relative in their will

If the lease is over 5 years, agricultural tenants can also:

- pass their tenancy on to a relative or spouse within their lifetime
- use the land for non-agricultural purposes

- Tenants with a 1991 Act tenancy have the right to buy the land they are leasing.

If there's a house on the land, both landlord and tenant have obligations to keep it in good repair.

Crofting tenancies

Crofting is a system of landholding unique to the Highlands and Islands of Scotland. Usually, the crofter holds the croft on the 'statutory conditions' and doesn't have a written lease. Crofting is regulated by the Crofting Commission. The tenant must get written agreement from the Commission if you want to make any changes to a crofting tenancy (including a change of tenant).

What the landlord must include in a tenancy agreement

If a landlord used an assured or short assured tenancy, the agreement must be written down. It must include:

- the names of all people involved
- the rental price and how it's paid
- the deposit amount and how it will be protected (see below)
- when the deposit can be fully or partly withheld (eg to repair damage caused by tenants)
- the property address
- the start and end date of the tenancy
- any tenant or landlord obligations
- who's responsible for minor repairs

- which bills your tenants are responsible for
- a statement telling the tenant that antisocial behaviour is a breach of the agreement

For other types of tenancy, it's still good practice to put the agreement in writing. including other information to avoid any confusion later, the landlord can include other information in the agreement, such as:

- whether the tenancy can be ended early and how this can be done
- information on how and when the rent will be reviewed
- whether the property can be let to someone else (sublet) or have lodgers

Changes to tenancy agreements

The landlord must get the agreement of their tenants if they want to make changes to the terms of their tenancy agreement.

Preventing discrimination

Unless the landlord has a very strong reason, they must change anything in a tenancy agreement that might discriminate against tenants on the grounds of:

- gender
- sexual orientation
- disability (or because of something connected with their disability)

- religion or belief
- being a transsexual person
- the tenant being pregnant or having a baby.

Ending a Short assured tenancy

Note the current eviction ban, as outlined above.

To get a property back, the landlord must give tenants a 'notice to quit' and a 'Section 33 notice'. For a short assured tenancy, the minimum notice period is 40 days if the tenancy is for 6 months or longer.

For a tenancy that is continuing on a month by month basis after the original period has ended, the notice period is a minimum of 28 days. The landlord must give 2 months notice when giving a Section 33 notice. They can issue both the notice to quit and Section 33 notice at the same time.

Other tenancy types (excluding the private residential tenancy)

For other tenancy types the landlord must give at least:

- 28 days if the tenancy is for up to 1 month
- 31 days if the tenancy is for up to 3 months
- 40 days if the tenancy is for more than 3 months.

Ending a tenancy early

A landlord can end a tenancy early if:

- the tenant breaks a condition of the tenancy agreement
- landlord and tenant agree to end the tenancy.

If tenants don't leave

If the notice period expires and tenants don't leave the property, the landlord can start the process of eviction through the courts. A landlord must tell tenants of their intention to get a court order by giving them a 'notice of intention to raise proceedings' (AT6) (see appendix).

If tenants want to leave

The tenancy agreement should say how much notice tenants need to give before they can leave the property.

If the notice isn't mentioned in the tenancy agreement, the minimum notice a tenant can give is:

- 28 days if their tenancy runs on a month-to-month basis (or if it's for less than a month)
- 40 days if their tenancy is for longer than 3 months.

Ending a tenancy early

Unless there's a break clause in the tenancy agreement, a landlord can insist that their tenants pay rent until the end of the tenancy. If tenants leave the property without giving notice, or before the notice has run out, they're still responsible for the property and the rent by law.

Houses in multiple occupation (HMOs)

If a tenant is living in a bedsit, shared flat, lodging, shared house, hostel or bed and breakfast accommodation it's likely that they will be living in a house in multiple occupation or 'HMO'. A landlord will have an HMO if:

- tenants live with two or more other people, and
- they don't belong to the same family, and
- they share some facilities, e.g., a bathroom or kitchen, and
- the accommodation is their only or main home (if they are a student, their term-time residence counts as their main home).

If they live with a homeowner their family doesnt count as 'qualifying persons' when deciding whether a property is an HMO. So, for example, if they share accommodation with the owner and one other unrelated lodger, they won't live in an HMO. If they live with the owner and two other unrelated lodgers, they will live in an HMO. Before the council gives a landlord an HMO licence, it will carry out the following checks:

Is the landlord a fit and proper person to hold a licence?

Before it grants an HMO licence, the council must check that the owner and anyone who manages the property (for example, a letting agent) don't have any criminal convictions, for example, for fraud or theft.

Is the property managed properly?

The council must check that the landlord respects tenants' legal rights. They should be given a written tenancy agreement stating clearly what the landlord's responsibilities are, and what the tenants responsibilities are. This should cover things like rent, repairs and other rules. To manage the property properly, the landlord must:

- keep the property and any furniture and fittings in good repair
- deal with the tenant fairly and legally when it comes to rent and other payments, for example they:
- must go through the correct procedure if they want to increase the rent
- cannot resell the tenant gas or electricity at a profit
- not evict the tenant illegally
- make sure that their tenants don't annoy or upset other people living in the area.

Does the property meet the required standards?

To meet the standards expected of an HMO property:

- the rooms must be a decent size, for example, every bedroom should be able to accommodate a bed, a wardrobe and a chest of drawers.
- there must be enough kitchen and bathroom facilities for the number of people living in the property, with adequate hot and cold water supplies.
- adequate fire safety measures must be installed, for example the landlord must provide smoke alarms and self-closing fire doors and make sure there is an emergency escape route.
- all gas and electrical appliances must be safe.
- heating, lighting and ventilation must all be adequate.

- the property should be secure, with good locks on the doors and windows.
- there must be a phone line installed so that tenants can set up a contract with a phone company to supply the service.

What are the landlord's responsibilities?

In order to keep their HMO licence, a landlord must maintain the property properly:

Common parts - these must be kept clean and in good repair (for example, the stairwell, hall, shared kitchen and bathroom). However, the landlord can include a clause in the tenancy agreement which passes this responsibility onto the tenants.

Shared facilities - these should be kept in good repair (for example, the cooker, boiler, fridge, sinks, bath and lighting).

Heating, hot water and ventilation - these facilities must all be kept in good order.

Gas safety - all gas appliances and installations must be safe (for example, a gas fire, boiler or cooker) - these should be checked once a year by a Gas Safe Register engineer

Electrical safety - all electrical appliances and installations must be safe - these should be tested every three years by a contractor approved by the National Inspection Council for Electrical

Installation Contracting (NICEIC) or SELECT, Scotland's trade association for the electrical, electronics and communications systems industry

Fire precautions - all fire precautions (for example, smoke alarms and fire extinguishers) must be in good working order and that the fire escape route is kept safe and free from obstructions.

Furniture - all furniture supplied must meet safety standards (for example, isn't flammable).

Roof, windows and exterior - these must all be adequately maintained.

Rubbish - enough rubbish bins must be provided.

Deposits - tenants' deposits must be returned within a reasonable time when they move out, preferably within 14 days.

The landlord should also put up notices in the accommodation giving the name and address of the person responsible for managing it so that the tenant can contact them whenever necessary explaining what the tenant should do in an emergency, for example if there is a gas leak or a fire.

Tenants' responsibilities:

Repairs – the tenant should let the landlord know if anything in the property needs repairing, particularly if this is something they are

hing the council

n suffering from domestic violence who has been forced to approach the local council and ask for help as a homeless Councils will demand proof of violence and you will need to ence from a professional person, such as a doctor or social or police. The council decides whether or not it has a duty to u and you should seek advice if they refuse. Some councils, all will offer help to battered women. If you are accepted as s then the council should not send you back to the area he violence began.

g a court order

course of action in an emergency is to obtain a court order he man you live with.

an issue orders stating that a man:

ld not assault you or harass you.
o assault any children living with you.
ave the home and not to return.
ep a certain distance from your home or any other place e your children go regularly.
t you back in your home if you have been excluded.

elieve a court order would help, you should get advice on find a solicitor or law centre that deals with these types of ons to the court. Certain orders are harder to get than

responsible for keeping in good order, such as the roof, boiler or toilet.

Damage – the tenant must take good care of the property and try not to damage anything.

Rubbish - not let rubbish pile up in or around the property but dispose of it properly in the bins provided.

Inspections - let the landlord inspect the property so they can check whether any maintenance work needs doing. Normally this should happen once every six months. The landlord must give you 24 hours' written notice before coming round.

Behave responsibly - make sure that the tenant doesnt behave in a way that can annoy or upset neighbours. The landlord is responsible for dealing with any complaints made by neighbours and must take action if they are unhappy with tenants' behaviour.

Safeguarding Tenancy Deposits

A tenancy deposit scheme is a scheme provided by an independent third party to protect deposits until they are due to be repaid.

Three schemes are now operating:
-Letting Protection Service Scotland
-Safedeposits Scotland
-Mydeposits Scotland

Landlord's legal duties

The legal duties on landlords who receive a tenancy deposit are:

- to pay deposits to an approved tenancy deposit scheme
- to provide the tenant with key information about the tenancy and deposit

Information about the schemes

Further details about the individual schemes are available on the individual scheme websites below. Email addresses and telephone numbers are also included. All three schemes have a range of information available for both landlords (and their agents) as well as tenants and these include how landlords can join the schemes, how to submit deposits, how to ask for repayment of deposits and how the dispute resolution service will work.

Letting Protection Service Scotland

www.lettingprotectionscotland.com

Email contact: events@lettingprotectionscotland.com

Telephone: 0330 303 0031

SafeDeposits Scotland

www.safedepositsscotland.com

Email contact: info@safedepositsscotland.com

Telephone: 0333 3213 136

Mydeposits Scotland

www.mydepositsscotland.co.uk

Email contact: info@mydepositsscotland.co.uk

Telephone: 0333 321 9402

Ch. 12

Relationship Breakdown anc

When a relationship breaks down, wheth
are married or not, problems can often
property that was home. The rights of pec
whether they are married or not, whe
partnership or whether there are childre
status of individuals in the home.

Housing rights in an emergency

In the main, it is women who suffer fror
section refers to women, but the rights ar
are a woman and have been threatened b
leave your home, then there are several p
emergency. The first of these is either gc
These provide shelter, advice and emotior
children. These refuges will always try to
are sometimes crowded. They will a
somewhere to live in the longer term.
telephone service if you need to find som
useful addresses at the back of this book.

Approa

A perso
flee can
person.
get evid
worker
help yo
but not
homeles
where t

Obtaini

Another
against

Courts c

- shou
- not
- to le
- to k whe
- to le

If you b
where t
applicat

others, such as exclusion orders. Matters need to be very serious indeed before such an order will be made. However, you will be advised of this when approaching a solicitor or law centre. Failure to obey the terms and conditions laid down in the order can lead to arrest for contempt and a fine or even imprisonment.

Long-term rights to the home

Long-term rights to stay in a home depend on a number of circumstances. If you are married or in a civil partnership and the ownership or tenancy of the property is in joint names you have equal rights to live in the property. If it is owned, then you will have a right to a share of the proceeds if it is sold. In certain circumstances you have a right to more (or less) than a half share, or to the tenancy in your name after divorce.

If you are married or in a civil partnership but the ownership or tenancy is in one name only there are laws to protect the rights of the other party. Courts have the power to decide who has the ownership or rights over the matrimonial home, even if the property is held in one person's name only. This can also apply to people who were married but are now divorced and to those who were planning to get married within three years of their engagement.

Spouses who are not the owner or tenant of the home have a right to stay there. The court has the power to exclude either of the spouses, even if they are sole or joint owner or tenant. If your husband has left and stopped paying the rent or mortgage payments, the landlord or building society is obliged to accept payments from you, if you wish to make them, even if the property is not in your name. If the home is owned by your husband, then you can register your right to live in it. This prevents your husband selling the home before the court has decided who should live there. And also prevents him taking out a second mortgage on the property without your knowledge. This is known as 'registering a charge' on the home. The court also has the power to transfer a fully protected private tenancy, an assured tenancy or a council or housing association tenancy from one partner to another.

If the matrimonial home is owner occupied and proceedings have started for a divorce, the court will decide how the value of the property will be divided up. The law recognises that, even if the property is in the husbands/civil partners name only, the wife/civil partner has a right to a share in its value, that she/he often makes a large unpaid contribution through housework or looking after children and that this should be recognised in divorce proceedings. The court looks at several things when reaching a decision:

- the income and resources of both partners.
- the needs of you and your husband.
- the standard of living that you and your husband had before the breakdown.
- ages of partners and length of marriage/civil partnership.
- contributions to the welfare of the family.
- conduct of partners.
- loss of benefits that you might have had if the marriage/civil partnership had not broken down.

The court also must consider whether there is any way that they can make a 'clean break' between you and your husband/civil partner so that there are no further financial ties between you. In certain circumstances, the court can order the sale of the matrimonial home and the distribution of proceeds between partners.

If you are not married or in a Civil Partnership

If you are not married/in a civil partnership, then your rights will depend on who is the tenant or the owner of the home.

Tenants

If a tenancy is in joint names, then you both have equal rights to the home. You can exclude your partner temporarily as we have seen by a court order. If you are a council tenant, then you may want to see if you can get the council to rehouse you. You should get advice on this from an independent agency (see useful addresses).

If the tenancy is in your partner's name only then the other person can apply for the right to stay there, for their partner to be excluded or for the tenancy to be transferred.

Homeowners

If you live in an owner occupied property you and your partner may have certain rights to a share of the property even if you are not married/in a civil partnership.

If the home is jointly owned, then you have a clear right to a share in its value. If one person has contributed more than the other, then a court can decide that an equal share is unfair. The court cannot order the transfer of the ownership of property, but it can order the sale and distribution of the proceeds.

If the home is in one person's name there is no automatic right to live in the home, even if there are children. However, a solicitor acting on your behalf can argue that by virtue of marriage/civil partnership and contribution you should be allowed to stay there and be entitled to a share.

****

Ch. 13

Housing Advice

General advice

Citizens Advice Bureaus, which are situated throughout the U.K., provide advice on all problems, including housing and other matters such as legal, welfare benefits and relationship breakdown. If appropriate they can refer you for more specialist help to a solicitor or advice agency. This advice is free of charge. To find a local office, look in the telephone directory under The National Association of Citizens Advice Bureau.

Government advice

Go to https://www.gov.uk/private-renting

This site gives detailed advice about the processes underpinning renting privately.

Tenants Voice

www.thetenantsvoice.co.uk/tenant-tools-and-resources/

This is an extremely useful site and offers advice on:

- Government Websites and Tools
- Housing / Legal Advice Services

- The Tenant's Voice Guides on Renting:
- Tenant Organizations Across The UK
- Landlord Accreditation Schemes and Regulatory Bodies
- Letting Agent Accreditation Schemes and Regulatory Bodies
- Letting Agent Redress Schemes
- Deposit Protection Schemes
- Renting Advice Websites and Housing Law Blogs
- Renting And Property Forums
- Landlord / Agent Rate and Review Websites
- Renting Tools and Services
- The Tenants' Voice Deals and Promotions

Housing Advice Centres

In many areas there are specialist advice centres offering housing aid and advice. The service they offer varies from one-off information to detailed help over a long period. There are two main types of housing advice centres, local council housing aid centres which can advise on all kinds of problems, although they will not be able to act against their own council and independent housing aid centres may be better equipped to do this.

These centres can offer detailed assistance over a length of time and also one-off advice. There are a number of independent housing aid centres throughout the country operated by Shelter.

You should contact Shelter for your nearest centre.

Other specialist advice

Law centers-they offer free advice and can sometimes represent you in court. They can usually advise on all aspects of law and also advise battered women. They cannot, however, take divorce cases. For this you will need a solicitor. Shelter can provide a list of law centers.

For advice on welfare rights, you should try the local council, who may employ a welfare rights advisor. Advisers can also contact the advice line which is run by the Child Poverty Action Group.

For women's rights the Women's Aid Federation England and Welsh Women's Aid refer battered women, with or without children, to refuges. They can put you in touch with sympathetic solicitors and local women's aid groups and can offer a range of other advice, such as welfare benefits.

For immigration advice, the Joint Council for the Welfare of Immigrants offers advice on all types of problems connected with immigration and nationality.

The United Kingdom Immigrants Advisory Service offers advice and help on problems with immigration. The Refugee Council has an advice service for refugees and asylum seekers.

Advice from solicitors

Solicitors can advise you on all aspects of the law, represent you in certain courts and, if necessary, get a barrister to represent you. It is best to find a solicitor who specialises in housing rights as they usually have a wider knowledge of specific areas. You can get a list of solicitors who specialise in housing law from the Community

Legal Service (CLS) Directory in your local library. The list is also on the CLS website. Citizens Advice Bureaus can also supply specialist solicitor details.

Free advice and help

The Legal Help Scheme, whilst also being squeezed, can pay for up to two hours worth of free advice and assistance and for matrimonial cases up to three hours. The scheme is means tested and you must come within the limits of the scheme to qualify. For details of the scheme, you should approach a Citizens Advice Bureau or a solicitor's practice operating the scheme. You must have reasonable grounds for defending an action. In certain cases, if you succeed in obtaining cash compensation then you may have to repay a proportion of it, this is known as the *statutory charge.*

****

Ch. 14

Agricultural Tenancies

If a person rents agricultural land or buildings to run a farm business, they may have an agricultural tenancy agreement. Every agricultural tenancy agreement is unique. We refer here to 2 types of agricultural tenancies governed by legislation:

- Farm Business Tenancies governed by the Agricultural Tenancies Act 1995 - those agreed after 1 September 1995
- 1986 Act Tenancies governed by the Agricultural Holdings Act 1986 - those agreed before 1 September 1995

Farm Business Tenancies

A tenancy is a Farm Business Tenancy if at least part of the tenanted land is farmed throughout the life of the tenancy. The tenancy must also meet one of these 2 conditions:

- if the tenancy is primarily agricultural to start with, the landlord and tenant can exchange notices before the tenancy begins confirming they intend it to remain a Farm Business Tenancy throughout - this lets tenants diversify away from agriculture where the terms of the tenancy agreement allow this.

- if the landlord and tenant don't exchange notices before the tenancy begins, the tenancy business must be primarily agricultural to be considered a Farm Business Tenancy

Farm Business Tenancy rent reviews

Landlords and tenants can negotiate their own rent levels and decide whether or not they want to have rent reviews. Either the landlord or tenant can demand a rent review every 3 years by law.

However, landlords and tenants can agree on how often a rent review should take place – this agreement replaces the law. For example, tenants can agree on a rent review every 4 years.

Farm Business Tenancy compensation

As a farm business tenant, a person is entitled to compensation at the end of a tenancy for:

- physical improvements they made to a holding (provided the landlord has given consent to the improvements)
- changes that increase the value of the holding (provided they are left behind when the tenant leaves)

Owners can agree in writing to an upper limit on the amount of compensation, usually equal to the tenant's cost in making the improvements.

Ending a Farm Business Tenancy

Landlords and tenants of a Farm Business Tenancy can end the tenancy by issuing a notice to quit. The minimum notice period to quit is 12 months.

1986 Act agricultural tenancies

Agricultural tenancies agreed before 1 September 1995 are known as 1986 Act Tenancies. They're also sometimes referred to as Full Agricultural Tenancies (FATs) or Agricultural Holdings Act tenancies (AHAs).

These tenancies usually have lifetime security of tenure and those granted before 12 July 1984 also carry statutory succession rights, on death or retirement. This means a close relative of a deceased tenant can apply for succession to the tenancy within 3 months of the tenant's death.

Applying for succession stops any notice to quit given by the landlord on the tenant's death. Two tenancies by succession can be granted, so it's possible for the tenant's family to work the holding for 3 generations. Farmers with a tenancy granted before 12 July 1984 can also name an eligible successor such as a close relative who can apply to take over the holding when they retire.

1986 Act Tenancies rent reviews

The landlord or tenant has the right to a rent review 3 years after either the:

- start of a tenancy
- previous rent review

If land is added to or removed from a holding, then the next rent review must be either at least 3 years from one of the following:

- the date the original tenancy began
- from the date of the previous rent review for the original tenancy

This rent review must happen even if the rent has changed to reflect changes to the amount of land on the holding.

1986 Act Tenancies compensation

Under the 1986 Act Tenancy agreements the tenant is entitled to compensation at the end of their tenancy for the following:

- major long-term improvements
- short-term improvements
- 'tenant right'

Major long-term improvements

These include:

- making or planting water meadows
- planting orchards
- erecting or altering buildings
- constructing silos, roads or bridges
- repairs to fixed equipment

Short-term improvements

These include:

- mole drainage
- protecting fruit trees against animals

- clay burning
- liming and chalking of land
- applying manure, fertiliser, soil improvers and digestate to the land (in England)

'Tenant right'

These include:

- the value of growing crops
- the costs of husbandry, such as sowing seeds and cultivations
- compensation for disturbance where a landlord terminates the tenancy with a notice to quit.

The amount of compensation is measured by the increase in value to the holding made by the improvements. The landlord may also claim compensation for disrepair - usually the cost of repairing any damage.

Dispute procedures

Where a landlord or a tenant has a dispute relating to an Agricultural Tenancy (either a 1986 Act Tenancy or a Farm Business Tenancy) they can use third-party expert determination or arbitration procedures.

Arbitration is the private legal settlement of a dispute by an independent, professional arbitrator which can involve either of the following:

- a tribunal hearing where both sides present evidence and testimony
- the 2 parties agreeing to resolve the dispute using written arbitration procedures, avoiding the time and costs of a hearing.

If a landlord and tenant can't agree on the appointment of an arbitrator, either of them can apply to the President of the Royal Institution of Chartered Surveyors (RICS) to make an appointment on their behalf for an arbitrator to:

- decide a rent review dispute
- resolve a dispute other than a rent review.

Contacts
Farmers can get further information on agricultural tenancy issues from the Tenant Farmers Association and the National Farmers Union. Please note that the law differs in Scotland and Wales, information on which can be obtained from these sites.

****

Chapter 15

Mobile Homes and Houseboats

Renting a mobile home

If you have a licence

Most people who rent a mobile home, such as a static caravan, have a licence to occupy rather than a tenancy. Your contract should tell you:

- how long you can stay
- how much notice you'll get
- your landlord's responsibilities

You still have some protection against eviction if you do not have a written agreement.

If you have a tenancy

Some people who rent a mobile home are tenants. You can only have a tenancy if your mobile home is classed as a 'dwelling house'. This might apply if it is:

- your home
- static and not able to be moved, even in two parts
- connected to mains supplies of electricity and water

If you're a tenant, your legal rights depend on the type of tenancy you have.

Eviction from a mobile home

You are usually entitled to at least 4 weeks' notice.

Your landlord must go to court and get a possession order to evict you from your home. You may be entitled to more notice and have additional protection from eviction if you have a tenancy.

Landlord harassment and illegal eviction

It's illegal for your landlord to harass you or force you to leave your mobile home. Harassment can include if your landlord:

- is abusive or violent
- cuts off your gas, electricity or water
- enters your home without your permission

There are steps you can take to deal with landlord harassment. The first likely port of call would be the Citizens Advice Bureau. The council can help if you're illegally evicted.

Repairs and conditions in mobile homes

Licensees

Your landlord is only responsible for repairs in your mobile home that are specified in your contract.

Tenants

Your landlord is responsible for most repairs in your mobile home. This usually includes:

- heating and hot water
- sinks, toilets, pipes and drains
- the roof and walls of your mobile home

Report repairs in writing to your landlord as soon as possible.

Claiming benefits for a mobile home

You can claim housing benefit or housing costs under universal credit if you have a low income or receive other benefits. It can be used to pay your rent or site fees.

Renting a houseboat

If you rent a boat, make sure it is rented to you with a residential mooring. Most all-year-round residential moorings do not allow boats to be rented out. Check that the site owner has given your landlord permission for you to stay there. The Canal and River Trust has more about renting a boat to live on.
www.canalandrivertrust.org.uk

Housing benefit and universal credit

If you're on a low income, you can usually get universal credit or housing benefit to help pay your:

- mooring fees
- a continuous cruiser licence
- rent if you do not own your boat

If you're working age and not getting housing benefit, you should apply for universal credit. You can apply for housing benefit if you're pension age.

Paying council tax for a houseboat

You may have to pay council tax if you live on a houseboat with a residential mooring.

Useful information on houseboats

Get legal advice if you're told you can no longer stay where you're moored.

Use the Law Society Directory to find legal help in your area. You can also contact the:

- National Bargee Travellers Association www.bargee-traveller.org.uk
- Canal & River Trust

****

GLOSSARY OF TERMS

FREEHOLDER: Someone who owns their property outright.

LEASEHOLDER: Someone who has been granted permission to live on someone else's land for a fixed term.

TENANCY: One form of lease, the most common types of which are fixed term or periodic.

LANDLORD: A person who owns the property in which the tenant lives.

LICENCE: A licence is an agreement entered into whereby the landlord is merely giving you permission to occupy his/her property for a limited period.

TRESPASSER: Someone who has no right through an agreement to live in a property.

PROTECTED TENANT: In the main, subject to certain exclusions, someone whose tenancy began before 15th January 1989.

ASSURED TENANT: In the main, subject to certain exclusions, someone whose tenancy began after 15th January 1989.

NOTICE TO QUIT: A legal document giving the protected tenant twenty eight days notice that the landlord intends to apply for possession of the property to the County Court.

GROUND FOR POSSESSION: One of the stated reasons for which the landlord can apply for possession of the property.

MANDATORY GROUND: Where the judge must give possession of the property.

DISCRETIONARY GROUND: Where the judge may or may not give possession, depending on his own opinion.

STUDENT LETTING: A tenancy granted by a specified educational institution.

HOLIDAY LETTING: A dwelling used for holiday purposes only.

ASSURED SHORTHOLD TENANCY: A fixed-term post-1989 tenancy.

PAYMENT OF RENT: Where you pay a regular sum of money in return for permission to occupy a property or land for a specified period.

FAIR RENT: A rent set by the Rent Officer every two years for most pre-1989 tenancies and which is lower than a market rent.

MARKET RENT: A rent deemed to be comparable with other non-fair rents in the area.

RENT ASSESSMENT COMMITTEE: A committee set up to review rents set by either the Rent Officer or the landlord.

PREMIUM: A sum of money charged for permission to live in a property.

DEPOSIT: A sum of money held against the possibility of damage to property.

QUIET ENJOYMENT: The right to live peacefully in your own Home.

REPAIRS: Work required to keep a property in good order.

IMPROVEMENTS: Alterations to a property.

LEGAL AID: Help with your legal costs, which is dependent on income.

HOUSING BENEFIT: Financial help with rent, which is dependent on income.

HOUSING ADVICE CENTRE: A center which exists to give advice on housing-related matters and which is usually local authority-funded.

LAW CENTRE: A center which exists for the purpose of assisting the public with legal advice.

****

Appendix 1 – Useful addresses

Age UK
Tavis House
1-6 Tavistock Square
London WC1 9NA
0800 055 6112
www.ageuk.org.uk

Child Poverty Action Group-England, Wales and Northern Ireland
30 Micawber Street
London N1 7TB
020 7837 7979
cpag.org.uk

Scotland
Unit 9, Ladywell Business Centre
94 Duke Street
Glasgow
G4 OUW
0141 552 3303

Consumers Association
2 Marylebone Road
London NW1 4DF
020 7770 7000
www.which.co.uk

Disability Rights UK
Plexal
14 East Bay Lane
Here East
Queen Elizabeth Olympic Park-
Stratford
London
E20 3BS
0330 995 0400
www.disabiliyrights.org

Gay and Lesbian Switchboard
switchboard.lgbt

Homeless Link
Minories House
2-5 Minories
London EC3N 1BJ
www.homeless.org.uk

Generation Rent
71 Howard Street
North Shields
NE30 1AF
www.generationrent.org

Legal Action Group
1st Floor 242 Pentonville Road
London
N1 9UN
020 7833 2931
www.lag.org.uk

Liberty
www.libertyhumanrights.org.uk

Shelter
Housing and Homeless Charity
www.england.shelter.org.uk
Will direct you to Shelter Scotland and Shelter Northern Ireland

Women's Aid Federation Helpline
www.womensaid.org.uk

Appendix 2

It should be noted that the enclosed sample agreements will be replaced in the summer of 2025, with the passage of the Renters Rights Bill 2024. The Grounds for Possession will also change.

Current sample Assured Shorthold Tenancy Agreement (England and Wales)

Current sample Section 21 Notice Requiring possession (FORM 6A)

For a wide range of other sample agreements covering all lets, including lodgers, the following sites are useful:

https://www.lawdepot.co.uk

https://www.rocketlawyer.com

There are numerous other sites providing either free agreements or paid documents.

****

ASSURED SHORTHOLD TENANCY AGREEMENT ENGLAND AND WALES

This Tenancy Agreement is between

Name and address of Landlord-

-AND

Name of tenant:

"

(in the case of Joint Tenants the term "Tenant" applies to each of them and the names of all Joint Tenants should be written above. Each Tenant individually has the full responsibilities and rights set out in this Agreement)

Address-in respect of:

("the Premises")

Description of Premises

-Which comprises of:

Term-The Tenancy is granted for a fixed term of [6] months

Date of start of tenancy-The Tenancy begins on:

(“The Commencement Date”) and is an assured shorthold monthly tenancy, the terms of which are set out in this Agreement.

Overcrowding-The Tenant agrees not to allow any person other than the Tenant to reside at the Premises.

Payment of Deposit-The Tenant agrees to pay on signing the Agreement a deposit of £ which will be returnable in full providing that the Landlord may deduct from such sums: The reasonable costs of any necessary repairs to the premises, building or common parts, or the replacement of any or all of the contents where such repair or replacement is due to any act or omission of the Tenant or family or visitors of the Tenant, such sums as are outstanding on leaving the Premises in respect of arrears or other charges including Court costs or other fees.

The deposit will be protected by The Deposit Protection Service (The DPS) in accordance with the Terms and Conditions of The DPS. The Terms and Conditions and ADR Rules governing the protection of the deposit including the repayment process can be found at www.depositprotection.com

Payment for the premises-

Rent: The rent for the premises is:

Service Charge:

Total:

In this Agreement the term "Rent" refers to the net rent and service charge set out above or as varied from time to time in accordance with this Agreement. The payment of monthly Rent is due in advance on the first Saturday of each month.
The service charge is in respect of the landlord providing the services listed in Schedule 1 to this Agreement for which the Tenant shall pay a service charge to be included in the rent. The service charge may be varied by the landlord in accordance with the terms set out in Schedule 1 to this Agreement.

I/We have read, understood and accept the terms and conditions contained within this agreement which include the standard terms and conditions attached.

Signed by the Tenant

.... Dated:

Signed on behalf of the landlord.
.... Dated:

If the Tenant feels that the landlord has broken this Agreement or not performed any obligation contained in it, he/she should first complain to the landlord in writing giving details of the breach or non-performance.

Terms and Conditions

1. It is agreed that:

Changes in Rent-1.1-The landlord may increase or decrease the Rent by giving the Tenant not less than 4 weeks notice in writing of the increase or decrease. The notice shall specify the Rent proposed. The first increase or decrease shall be on the first day of following the Commencement Date of this Agreement. Subsequent increases or decreases in the Rent shall take effect on the first day of in each subsequent year. The revised Rent shall be the amount specified in the notice of increase unless the Tenant exercises his/her right to refer the notice to a Rent Assessment Committee to have a market rent determined in which case the maximum Rent payable for one year after the date specified in the notice shall be the Rent so determined.

Altering the Agreement-1.2-With the exception of any changes in Rent, this Agreement may only be altered by the agreement in writing of both the Tenant and the landlord.

2. The landlord agrees:

Possession-2.1-To give the Tenant possession of the Premises at the commencement of the Tenancy.

Tenant's Right to Occupy-2.2-Not to interrupt or interfere with the Tenant's right peacefully to occupy the Premises except where:

(i) access is required to inspect the condition of the Premises or to carry out repairs or other works to the Premises or adjoining property; or

(ii) a court has given the Association possession by ending the Tenancy.

Repair of Structure and Exterior-2.3-To keep in good repair the structure and exterior of the Premises including:

(i) drains, gutters and external pipes;

(ii) the roof;

(iii) outside wall, outside doors, windowsills, window catches, sash cords and window frames including necessary external painting and decorating;

(iv) internal walls, floors and ceilings, doors and door frames, door hinges and skirting boards but not including internal painting and decoration;

(v) plasterwork;

(vi) chimneys, chimney stacks and flues but not including sweeping;

(vii) pathways, steps or other means of access;

(viii) integral garages and stores;

(ix) boundary walls and fences.

Repair of Installations-2.4-To keep in good repair and working order any installations provided by the landlord for space heating, water heating and sanitation and for the supply of water, gas and electricity including:

(i) basins, sinks, baths, toilets, flushing systems and waste pipes;

(ii) electric wiring including sockets and switches, gas pipes and water pipes;

(iii) water heaters, fireplaces, fitted fires and central heating installations

Repair of Common Parts-2.5-To take reasonable care to keep the common entrances, halls, stairways, lifts, passageways, rubbish chutes and any other common parts, including their lighting, in reasonable repair and fit for use by the Tenant and other occupiers and visitors to the Premises.

External & Internal
Decorations-2.6-To keep the exterior and interior of the Premises and any common parts in a good state of decoration and normally to decorate these areas once every 5 years.

3. The Tenant agrees:
Possession-3.1-To take possession of the Premises at the commencement of the Tenancy and not to part with possession of the Premises or sub-let the whole or part of it.

Rent-3.2-To pay the Rent monthly and in advance. The first payment shall be made on the signing of the Agreement in respect of the period from the Commencement Date to the first Saturday of the following month.

Use of Premises-3.3-To use the Premises for residential purposes as the Tenant's only or principal home and not to operate a business at the Premises without the written consent of the landlord.

Nuisance and Racial and other Harassment-3.4-Not to behave or allow members of his/her household or any other person visiting the Premises with the Tenant's permission to behave in a manner nor do anything which is likely to be a nuisance to the tenants, owners or lessees of any of the other properties or other persons lawfully visiting the property. In particular, not to cause any interference, nuisance or annoyance through noise, anti-social behaviour or threats of or actual violence or any damage to property belonging to the said persons. This Clause also applies to any conduct or activity which amounts to harassment including: abuse and intimidation, creating unacceptable levels of noise or causing intentional damage or any other persistent behaviour which causes offence, discomfort or inconvenience on the grounds of colour, race religion, sex, sexual orientation and disability.

Noise-3.5-Not to play or allow to be played any radio, television, audio equipment or musical instrument so loudly that it causes a nuisance or annoyance to neighbours or can be heard outside the Premises.

Domestic Violence-3.6-Not to use or threaten violence against any other person living in the Premises such that they are forced to leave by reason of the Tenant's violence or fear of such violence.

Pets-3.7-To keep under control any animals at the Premises and to obtain the written consent of the landlord before keeping a dog or any other animal.

Car Repairs-3.8-That no car servicing or car repairs shall be carried out in the roads or accessway or parking spaces or in the forecourt or approaches to the Premises, such as to be a nuisance or annoyance to neighbours.

Paraffin-3.9-Not to use any paraffin or bottled gas heating, lighting or cooking appliances on the Premises nor any appliances which discharge the products of combustion into the interior of the Premises.

Vehicles-3.10-That no commercial vehicle, caravan, boat, or lorry shall be parked in the accessway or parking spaces (regardless of whether this forms part of the Premises) or in the forecourt or approaches to the Premises or the adjoining premises.

Keeping premises clean-3.11-To keep the interior of the Premises in a clean condition. The Tenant agrees to return the property in the same decorative order as at the start of the tenancy taking into account fair wear and tear.

Damage-3.12-To make good any damage caused willfully or by neglect or carelessness on the part of the Tenant or any member of the Tenant's household or visitor to the Premises including the replacement of any broken glass in windows and repair or replacement of any damaged fittings and installations. If the Tenant fails to make good any damage for which he/she is responsible the landlord may enter the Premises and carry out the work in default and the cost of this work shall be recoverable by the Association from the Tenant.

Reporting Disrepair-3.13-To report to the landlord any disrepair or defect for which the landlord is responsible in the structure or exterior of the Premises or in any installation therein or in the common parts.

Access-3.14-To allow the landlords employees or contractors acting on behalf of the landlord access at all reasonable hours of the daytime to inspect the condition of the Premises or to carry out repairs or other works to the Premises or adjoining property. The landlord will normally give at least 24 hours' notice, but immediate access may be required and shall be given in an emergency.

Assignment-3.15-Not to assign the Tenancy.

Sub-Tenants-3.16-Not to sub-let the whole or part of the Premises.

Ending the Tenancy-3.17-To give the landlord at least [4] weeks notice in writing when the Tenant wishes to end the Tenancy.

Moving Out-3.18-To give the landlord vacant possession and return the keys of the Premises at the end of the Tenancy and to remove all personal possessions and rubbish and leave the Premises and the landlords furniture and fixtures in good lettable condition and repair. The landlord accepts no responsibility for anything left at the Premises by the Tenant at the end of the Tenancy.

4. The Tenant has the following rights:

Right to Occupy-4.1-The Tenant has the right to occupy the Premises without interruption or interference from the landlord for the duration of this Tenancy (except for the obligation contained in this Agreement to give access to the landlord's employees or contractors) so long as the Tenant complies with the terms of this Agreement and has proper respect for the rights of other tenants and neighbours.

Security of Tenure-4.2-The Tenant has security of tenure as an assured tenant so long as he/she occupies the Premises as his/her only or principal home. Before the expiry of the fixed term the landlord can only end the Tenancy by obtaining a court order for possession of the Premises on one of the grounds listed in Schedule 2 of the Housing Act 1988. The landlord will only use the following grounds to obtain an order for possession:
--The tenant has not paid rent which is due; (Ground 10)
The Tenant has broken, or failed to perform, any of the conditions of this Tenancy; (Ground 12)
The Tenant or anyone living in the premises has caused damage to, or failed to look after the premises, the building, any of the common parts; (Ground 13)

The Tenant or anyone living in the premises has caused serious or persistent nuisance or annoyance to neighbours, or has been responsible for any act of harassment on the grounds of race, colour, religion, sex, sexual orientation, or disability, or has been convicted of using the property for immoral or illegal purposes; (Ground 14) or because of domestic violence (Ground 14A)
Where the tenancy has devolved under the will or intestacy of the Tenant
Suitable alternative accommodation is available to the Tenant.

Notice Periods for ending Assured Tenancy-4.3-Before the expiry of the fixed term the landlord agrees that it will not give less than four weeks notice in writing of its intention to seek a possession order except where it is seeking possession on Ground 14 or Ground 14A (whether or not combined with other Grounds) where it shall give such period of notice that it shall decide and that is not less than the statutory minimum notice period

Expiry of Tenancy-4.4-The landlord can only end the Tenancy by giving the Tenant at least two months notice that it requires possession of the Premises and by obtaining a court order for possession. The court will make an order for possession if it is satisfied that the proper notice has been given.

Cessation of Assured Tenancy-4.5-If the Tenancy ceases to be an assured tenancy the landlord may end the Tenancy by giving four weeks' notice in writing which shall be validly served on the Tenant if posted or delivered to the Premises.

**

Department for
Communities and
Local Government

FORM 6A
Notice seeking possession of a property let on an Assured Shorthold Tenancy

Housing Act 1988 section 21(1) and (4) as amended by section 194 and paragraph 103 of Schedule 11 to the Local Government and Housing Act 1989 and section 98(2) and (3) of the Housing Act 1996

Please write clearly in black ink. Please tick boxes where appropriate.

This form should be used where a no fault possession of accommodation let under an assured shorthold tenancy (AST) is sought under section 21(1) or (4) of the Housing Act 1988.

There are certain circumstances in which the law says that you cannot seek possession against your tenant using section 21 of the Housing Act 1988, in which case you should not use this form. These are:

(a) during the first four months of the tenancy (but where the tenancy is a replacement tenancy, the four month period is calculated by reference to the start of the original tenancy and not the start of the replacement tenancy – see section 21(4B) of the Housing Act 1988);

(b) where the landlord is prevented from retaliatory eviction under section 33 of the Deregulation Act 2015;

(c) where the landlord has not provided the tenant with an energy performance certificate, gas safety certificate or the Department for Communities and Local Government's publication "How to rent: the checklist for renting in England" (see the Assured Shorthold Tenancy Notices and Prescribed Requirements (England) Regulations 2015);

(d) where the landlord has not complied with the tenancy deposit protection legislation; or

(e) where a property requires a licence but is unlicensed.

Landlords who are unsure about whether they are affected by these provisions should seek specialist advice.

This form must be used for all ASTs created on or after 1 October 2015 except for statutory periodic tenancies which have come into being on or after 1 October 2015 at the end of fixed term ASTs created before 1 October 2015. There is no obligation to use this form in relation to ASTs created prior to 1 October 2015, however it may nevertheless be used for all ASTs.

What to do if this notice is served on you

You should read this notice very carefully. It explains that your landlord has started the process to regain possession of the property referred to in section 2 below.

You are entitled to at least two months' notice before being required to give up possession of the property. However, if your tenancy started on a periodic basis without any initial fixed term a longer notice period may be required depending on how often you are required to pay rent (for example, if you pay rent quarterly, you must be given at least three months' notice, or, if you have a periodic tenancy which is half yearly or annual, you must be given at least six months' notice (which is the maximum)). The date you are required to leave should be shown in section 2 below. After this date the landlord can apply to court for a possession order against you.

Where your tenancy is terminated before the end of a period of your tenancy (e.g. where you pay rent in advance on the first of each month and you are required to give up possession in the middle of the month), you may be entitled to repayment of rent from the landlord under section 21C of the Housing Act 1988.

If you need advice about this notice, and what you should do about it, take it immediately to a citizens' advice bureau, a housing advice centre, a law centre or a solicitor.

1. To:

   Name(s) of tenant(s) (Block Capitals)

2. You are required to leave the below address after [ ] [1]. If you do not leave, your landlord may apply to the court for an order under section 21(1) or (4) of the Housing Act 1988 requiring you to give up possession.

   Address of premises

1 Landlords should insert a calendar date here. The date should allow sufficient time to ensure that the notice is properly served on the tenant(s). This will depend on the method of service being used and landlords should check whether the tenancy agreement makes specific provision about service. Where landlords are seeking an order for possession on a periodic tenancy under section 21(4) of the Housing Act 1988, the notice period should also not be shorter than the period of the tenancy (up to a maximum of six months), e.g. where there is a quarterly periodic tenancy, the date should be three months from the date of service.

3. This notice is valid for six months only from the date of issue unless you have a periodic tenancy under which more than two months' notice is required (see notes accompanying this form) in which case this notice is valid for four months only from the date specified in section 2 above.

4. Name and address of landlord

To be signed and dated by the landlord or their agent (someone acting for them). If there are joint landlords each landlord or the agent should sign unless one signs on behalf of the rest with their agreement.

Signed | *Date* (DD/MM/YYYY)

Please specify whether: ☐ landlord ☐ joint landlords ☐ landlord's agent

Name(s) of signatory/signatories (Block Capitals)

Address(es) of signatory/signatories

Telephone of signatory/signatories

Department for
Communities and
Local Government

Notice seeking possession of a property let on an Assured Shorthold Tenancy (Form 6a)

This form should be used where a no fault possession of accommodation let under an assured shorthold tenancy (AST) is sought under section 21(1) or (4) of the Housing Act 1988.

This form must be used for all ASTs created on or after 1 October 2015 except for statutory periodic tenancies which have come into being on or after 1 October 2015 at the end of fixed term ASTs created before 1 October 2015.

The validity period of this form is six months following the date of its issue unless the tenancy is a periodic tenancy under which more than two months' notice is required, in which case the validity period is four months from the date the tenant is required to leave (see notes accompanying the form).

You cannot use this form:

in the first four months of the tenancy (but where the tenancy is a replacement tenancy, the four month period is calculated by reference to the start of the original tenancy and not the start of the replacement tenancy – see section 21(4B) of the Housing Act 1988);

where the landlord is prevented from retaliatory eviction under section 33 of the Deregulation Act 2015;

where the landlord has not provided the prescribed information and/or prescribed documents as set out below;

where the landlord has not complied with the tenancy deposit protection legislation; or

where a property requires a licence but is unlicensed.

Prescribed Information

The landlord is required to provide a copy of the Department for Communities and Local Government's publication "How to rent: the checklist for renting in England" by providing a pdf copy (which may be obtained from www.gov.uk/government/publications/how-to-rent). We recommend that this should be given at the start of the tenancy. Landlords are not required to supply a further copy of the publication each time a different version is published during the tenancy.

Where the landlord has failed to provide the publication, this form may not be used. However, this restriction is lifted as soon as the publication has been provided.

The requirement does not apply where a landlord is a private registered provider of social housing or where a landlord has already provided the tenant with an up-to-date version of the booklet under an earlier tenancy.

If the tenant has not notified the landlord, or a person acting on behalf of the landlord, of an e-mail address at which the tenant is content to accept service of notices and other documents given under or in connection with the tenancy, the landlord must provide a paper copy of the publication.

Prescribed documents:

Where the landlord has failed to comply with certain existing legal obligations, this form may not be used. However, this restriction is lifted as soon as the obligations have been complied with. The obligations are the requirement on a landlord to provide the tenant with:

- an Energy Performance Certificate (Reg 6(5), The Energy Performance of Buildings (England and Wales) Regulations 2012); and
- a gas safety certificate (Reg 36(6)(a), The Gas Safety (Installation and Use) Regulations 1998)

Tenants that need advice about this notice, and what to do about it, should take it immediately to a citizens' advice bureau, a housing advice centre, a law centre or a solicitor.

Tenants can also get expert, independent advice free from Shelterline on 0808 800 4444. Their advisers will be able to give expert advice, independent advice.

Index

Abolition of rental bidding, 62
Abolition of Section 21, 61
Accelerated (Fast-track) possession, 8, 112
Accidents, 94
Assured shorthold tenancy, 63

Banning orders, 24
Banning Orders, 23
Bedsits, 3, 45

Carbon Monoxide Alarm (England) Regulations 2015, 95, 96
Company lets, 3, 43

Damages, 6, 82, 87
Deposit, 3, 38, 39, 115
Deposits, 3, 38
Disabled tenants, 7, 89
Discretionary grounds for possession, 66

Electrical Equipment (Safety) Regulations 1994, 100
Electrical Safety, 7, 100
Ending a tenancy, 4, 59
Eviction, 6, 79, 81

Fire Extinguishers, 7, 97

Fire Safety Order 2005, 95, 101
Fire Safety Regulations, 7, 95
Freehold, 4, 56
Furniture, 7, 98, 107

Gas Appliances(Safety) Regulations 1995, 98
Gas Cooking Appliances (safety) Regulations 1989, 98
Gas safety, 7, 98
Gas safety (Installation and use) Regulations 1998, 98
Generation Rent, 14, 166
Ghost landlords, 29

Heating Appliances(Fireguard) (safety) Regulations 1991, 98
Holiday lets, 3, 45
Home owners, 10, 145
Houseboats, 11, 157
Houses in Multiple Occupation, 45
Housing Act 1985, 85
Housing Act 1988, 73
Housing Act 2004, 45, 85
Housing Advice Centres, 10, 148
Housing rights in an emergency, 10, 141

Implied standards of fitness for human habitation, 6, 85
Injunction, 81
Insurance, 8, 108

Kindroom, 4, 48, 49

Landlords obligations, 4, 59
Law centres, 149
Leasehold, 4, 56

Mandatory grounds for possession, 64
Mobile Homes, 11, 157

Obtaining a court order, 10, 142
Overcrowding, 4, 63

Pandemic, 55, 83
PAT test, 102
Periodic tenancies, 18
Plugs and Sockets etc. (Safety) Regulations 1994., 101
Protected tenancies, 63
Protection from Eviction Act 1977, 79

Rent Assessment Committee, 74
Rent control, 73
Rent increases, 20, 62, 123
Rent Officer, 73, 74, 162, 163
Rent Repayment Orders, 25
Rental guarantees, 3, 41
Renters Reform Bill, 14
Repairs, 6, 83

Reporting repairs, 7, 88
Residential Property Tribunal., 87
Rogue Landlord Database, 23

Sanitation, 8, 105
Scotland, 31, 122
Security of tenure, 5, 64
Services, 4, 59
Student lets, 3, 44

Tenancy Deposit Protection Scheme, 3, 38
Tenants obligations, 4, 59
The contract, 4, 58
The Electrical Safety Standards in the Private Rented Sector (England) Regulations 2020., 100
The Renters Rights Bill, 3, 14, 36
The tenancy agreement, 4, 57, 59, 108

Unlawful eviction, 24

****